NAMIBIA

NAMIBIA

Land of Tears, Land of Promise

Roy J. Enquist

Selinsgrove: Susquehanna University Press
London and Toronto: Associated University Presses

Associated University Presses
440 Forsgate Drive
Cranbury, NJ 08512

Associated University Presses
25 Sicilian Avenue
London WC1A 2QH, England

Associated University Presses
P.O. Box 488, Port Credit
Mississauga, Ontario
Canada L5G 4M2

The paper used in this publication meets the requirements
of the American National Standard for Permanence of Paper
for Printed Library Materials Z39.48-1984.

Library of Congress Cataloging-in-Publication Data

Enquist, Roy J.
  Namibia : land of tears, land of promise / Roy J. Enquist.
    p. cm.
  Includes bibliographical references.
  ISBN 0-945636-09-1 (alk. paper)
  1. Christianity—Namibia. 2. Namibia—History. I. Title.
BR1458.E57 1990
276.881—dc20   88-43395
                                          CIP

PRINTED IN THE UNITED STATES OF AMERICA

Contents

Foreword

Namibia: Land of Tears, Land of Promise represents a study that is both significant and timely.

It is significant because it delineates with skill and care the history of a people who have shown extraordinary courage in seeking to free themselves, first, from the bondage of crass and brutal nineteenth-century colonialism, and then from the terrorism of twentieth-century racism as it is manifested in the apartheid system of South Africa.

It is timely because there is once more considerable hope that this people may have their chance to become free under the plan of the United Nations that provides for free elections in that territory and the establishment of a free and independent government. Implementation of U.N. Resolution 435 has been ten years in coming. If all goes well, the process of implementation might begin while this book is still at the printers. If it fails to be implemented once again, because of the intransigence of the Republic of South Africa, then the struggle to become a free and independent country will continue. As Anglican Bishop James Kauluma of Namibia has often said, "We are slaves of hope."

Yet, far more than being an important historical examination coming at the right time, this book seeks to interpret a remarkable phenomenon. It may be summarized with the provocative question that the author has posed: "Can one preach a theology of the cross and, at the same time, be a freedom fighter?" How is is possible that the Christian churches of that area, especially the conservative Lutheran churches to which more than half of the population belongs, have been able to play such a decisive role in the struggle for freedom and human rights in Namibia? Coming out of a missionary enterprise that had deep roots in nineteenth-century German and Finnish pietism, and was itself often ambiguous with regard to oppression and exploitation of the colonial policies of Germany, we see the churches playing a leading role in the movement to liberate the people from their bondage. Furthermore, we find creative liberation theology emanating from a theology that

7

had often enough misunderstood and misused Luther's doctrine of the two Kingdoms.

That, in itself, is important enough, but Roy J. Enquist points out with clarity the lesson we may learn from the experience of the churches of Namibia. It raises poignant questions with regard to the church in the face of oppression, exploitation, and deprivation. When is the church guilty of complicity in the social injustice and the violation of human rights that are found in most nations of the world?

Himself a scholar of high standing and broad experience, Enquist is well qualified to write this book. Almost from the beginning of his career as a theologian he has been a popular and able teacher of the church. He is Professor of Theology and Ethics at the Lutheran Theological Seminary at Gettysburg, Pennsylvania, and director of the seminary's House of Studies in Washington, D.C. Previously, he served as campus pastor at the University of Chicago and at the Illinois Institute of Technology, as Assistant Professor at Wittenberg University in Springfield, Ohio, and as Professor at Texas Lutheran College. His experience as Visiting Professor at Marang Lutheran Seminary, Rustenburg, South Africa, in 1975 and 1976, which also brought him to the Paulinum Theological Seminary in Namibia, left a lasting mark. It is out of this experience and his continuing commitment to Namibian independence that Dr. Enquist writes this important book.

I am happy to commend this book to the reader because it also demonstrates the importance of seeing the mission of the Church in a global perspective. Without question, the churches of Namibia have been aided and supported by the global community of churches in their ongoing struggle, and continue to call for such help and support. At the same time, these churches have provided inspiration and strength to the Christian community of churches throughout the world as they face the challenges of their mission. Roy Enquist has caught this important ecclesiological fact in his book. For this reason, the book will also be of great service to the global community of churches as they participate in the struggle of the churches of Namibia.

Carl H. Mau, Jr.
Former General Secretary
Lutheran World Federation

Preface

This investigation has grown out of a scarcely credible discovery begun a decade ago when Zephania Kameeta, then president of the Paulinum Seminary in Namibia, invited me to visit and lecture at his school. It was at Otjimbingwe, site of the seminary and one-time capital of the country, that I first became aware of a historical curiosity: the two churches that support Paulinum represent a tradition of nineteenth-century pietism, which now provides major religious support for the political liberation of the Namibian people. How did these large conservative churches, traditionally regarded as apolitical, come to be standard-bearers in an emerging nation's struggle for independence? Pietistic religion can be politically active, as Poland reminds us. The Polish church, however, only needs to preserve a traditional national identity in the face of a new threat from an ancient foe. But Namibia can hardly be said to have had a national identity until very recently. Its churches, in the face of a complex history of successive imperialisms, have chosen to break with traditional political loyalties in an effort to create a national identity where none had existed before.

It is not difficult to see how Marxist analysis can serve the anti-imperialist concerns of liberation theologians in Latin America. But is it believable that nineteenth-century pietism, transplanted to Africa, could generate a religiously profound liberationist posture? The social ethic of the Namibian churches does not conform to the assumptions of the West. It contradicts our perceptions of what religion can do. Namibian Christians appear to have found in the Word of God, brought to them primarily from Germany and Finland, a message of such comprehension as to be unknown in popular religion elsewhere, and indeed largely unrecognized in academic theology.

The clash of dogmas, Alfred North Whitehead once observed, is not a tragedy but an opportunity. The novelty that the Namibian struggle presents requires an examination of the particular historical context that has enabled its pietism to behave so strangely. It will also oblige us to examine the substance of this new shape of evangelical ethics. Has this political activism been purchased at the

cost of a loss of religious integrity? Is this new political engagement
a child born of mere expediency? Perhaps pragmatic religion is no
more inevitably unprincipled than introverted piety is necessarily
high-minded. But the problem remains: Does Namibian ethics
operate with integrity, or is it but an improvisation under pressure,
understandable for all of that, but finally ephemeral?

Questions about context and substance require careful attention.
The first two chapters trace the main contours of the Namibian
story, an unfamiliar tale to most Westerners, a legacy in which
empires and churches grope in a brutal struggle between indigenous and colonial people. A final chapter attempts to engage the
reader in theological reflection on the meaning of the Namibian
ethic that has emerged. Here we see African theology that rises
from the life of a people in travail. We see something of the consequences of believing that the Word of God is not primarily a
collection of documents, but a sustaining presence in a history of
sorrow, a word that connects human misery and human hope with a
God of inexhaustible grace. In Africa everything in creation is
connected to everything else so that finally nothing is foreign to
God's presence. But just how both politics and piety can share in
that connectedness and thus both be central to God's kingdom
needs to be explored.

This study would not have been possible without the constant
support and encouragement of my wife, Mia Ingeborg Enquist, who
not only served with me at the Marang Lutheran Theological Seminary in Rustenberg, South Africa, in 1975 and 1976 when I was able
to make my first visit to Namibia, but who has been a source of
invaluable and wise counsel in this present project. In our life's
journey together she has been my dear companion, gracious and
loving beyond measure.

A number of people have been of great assistance in the gathering
of the materials that follow. In Namibia itself a variety of church
leaders gave generously of time and interest: Kleopas Dumeni and
Hendrik Frederik, bishops of the Evangelical Lutheran churches in
South West Africa/Namibia, and their staffs in Oniipa and Wind-
hoek, respectively; James Kauluma, Anglican Bishop of Namibia;
Fr. H. Henning, O.M.I., Vicar General of the Roman Catholic
Diocese of Windhoek; Dieter Schuetter, pastor of Christ Church,
Windhoek; and Abisai Shejavali, General Secretary of the Council
of Churches of Namibia. I'm also indebted to Zephania Kameeta,
auxiliary bishop fo the Evangelical Lutheran Church in South West
Africa/Namibia (Rhenish Mission). It was when I was the guest of

his family at the Paulinum Seminary that I was first introduced to the sorrow and hope, which is the Namibian story.

I also want to express my appreciation to the Lutheran Theological Seminary at Gettysburg, for granting me a sabbatical leave and the Lutheran Brotherhood for financial support that made my second visit to Namibia possible. Particularly helpful were the staff of the Lutheran World Ministries Office of World Community, Edward C. May and his successor, Ralston Deffenbaugh. The initial version of this study profited from the valuable criticism of Paul Isaak, a Namibian pastor engaged in doctoral studies at the Lutheran School of Theology at Chicago, and Professor William H. Jennings of Muhlenberg College, Allentown, Pennsylvania. I am also grateful to Carol J. Johnson for her expert assistance in preparing these pages for the publisher.

Acknowledgments

The author gratefully acknowledges permission to reprint excerpts from:

Two Kingdoms and One World by Karl H. Hertz, copyright © 1976 Augsburg Publishing House.

Appeal to Lutheran Christians in Southern Africa Concerning the Unity and the Witness of Lutheran Churches and Their Members in Southern Africa, Federation of the Evangelical Lutheran Churches in Southern Africa, 1975.

The Lutheran Teaching on the Two Kingdoms, edited by Gunnar Listerud, 1967 Lutheran Theological Seminary, Republic of South Africa.

Zeischen Kultur und Politik by Theo Sundermeier, copyright © 1978 Lutherisches Verlagshaus, Hannover.

Namibia, the Story of a Bishop in Exile by Colin Winter, copyright © 1977 Lutterworth Press, Cambridge, U.K.

Mission and Colonialism by J. L. de Vries, n.d., Raven Press, Bramfontein, Republic of South Africa.

The Revolt of the Hereros by Jon M. Bridgman, copyright © 1981 University of California Press.

Christus, Der Schwarze Befreier by Theo Sundermeier, copyright © 1973 Verlag der Evangelisch-Lutherischen Mission, Erlangen.

The maps and photographs from the International Defence and Aid Fund, London, are also reprinted with permission.

NAMIBIA

1
Tribes and Empires

Even today the population of the wildly beautiful "land that God made in anger" is not sizable: some 1,250,000 Namibians live in a country the size of California, Oregon, and Washington combined.[1] Denizens of the sixth wealthiest nation in Africa, inheritors of so spacious a land, would appear to be among the most favored of the children of God. Most of the recorded history of the land now called Namibia has been, however, the narrative of tears. In the belief that the past need not be a prologue, Namibians and those of their friends who have been captivated by one of Africa's most tragic tales now look for signs of hope that would break through the anger so bountifully displayed in both landscape and history.

It would be false to claim that the Namibians lived in an Eden before the arrival of the Europeans. And yet, the Western civilization transplanted to this new land found itself free to demonstrate the best and the worst Europe could imagine. Successive colonialisms would fight among themselves both militarily and ideologically. But in the matters that count they would not question their consensus: they who have the power, and the will, to rule will do so for their own benefit; the indigenous population, accordingly, is never to be permitted to be, in the African idiom, "a master in its own house." Thus, the policies of the empires, both German and British, and that of South African colonialism as well, have demonstrated remarkable continuity when dealing with the people and politics of southwestern Africa.

In spite of itself, the European presence in Namibia has managed to leave a legacy it now only vaguely understands itself, a deposit of religious faith that carries hidden within itself the potentiality for subverting all oppressions. This faith, intended by some to quiet the inhabitants of the land, has now proven unpredictable. Within a mere century, it has come to provide both catalyst and energy for nothing less than a fundamental reconstruction of the nation's identity. Perhaps this should have been anticipated. After all, religious faith, as the West has had ample time to learn, is capable both

17

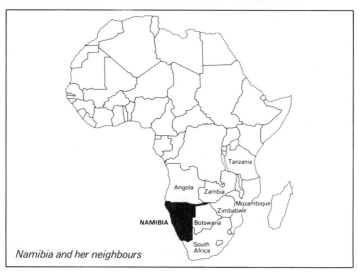

Namibia and her neighbours

(Courtesy of IDAF.)

of promising the gift of freedom and arousing the deepest of hungers for it. Freedom, born of faith, cannot be long confined to "otherworldly" realms—least of all in incorrigibly holistic Africa. Africans can only ask: If God has made us free, why are we still in bondage? Religious faith, sometimes seen as the great reconciler of the oppressed to their oppressions, is also capable of serving as the fundamental subverter of structures that violate faith's promise.

The Namibian story, only dimly known beyond its home, is a tale both of oppression and of hope. It is a narrative of guns and Bibles, of infamous barbarism and intellectual imagination. But since the political destiny of the land is still largely in the control of foreign powers, international ignorance regarding its plight serves to reinforce its oppression and to postpone its liberation. This study is interested in bringing to light key elements in the Namibian story, partly to help make more generally known the remarkable record of a beleaguered people, and partly to consider whether their hard-won understanding of faith may not speak to a world increasingly aware of the seriousness of its own moral plight.

The First Settlers

The West has known of Namibia, one way or another, for half a millennium. In 1485 the Portuguese navigator Diago Cao, seeking a sea route to India, stumbled onto the sandy, rocky wastes of

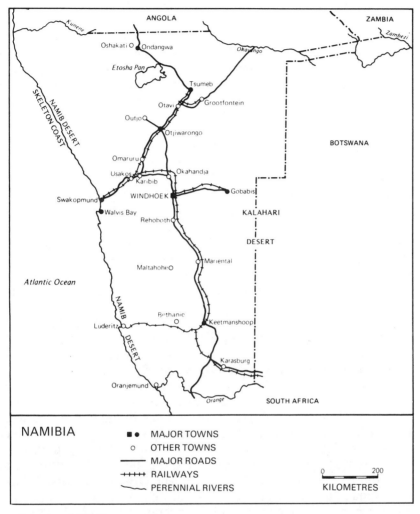

NAMIBIA

■● MAJOR TOWNS
○ OTHER TOWNS
— MAJOR ROADS
+++++ RAILWAYS
⌇ PERENNIAL RIVERS

0   200
KILOMETRES

(Courtesy of IDAF.)

Namibia's Atlantic shore. It would later be aptly dubbed the Skeleton Coast. Long before, the first inhabitants of the territory, the San (the so-called Bushmen) maintained their Stone Age culture in small scattered groups across southern Africa, including portions of what would later be called Namibia. Subsequently, much larger groups measuring their wealth in domesticated cattle entered the area in three major phases.

From about A.D. 1000 to 1200 Nama (the so-called Hottentots) slowly moved down the westerly portion of the land toward the south, crossing the Orange River into what is now the Cape Province of the Republic of South Africa. Between 1400 and 1500 four major groups also drifed into the country from the north: the Ovambo, the Kavango, the Herero, and the Damara. The first two remained in the north and northeast areas respectively, while the others continued further south into the central portion of the country, struggling among themselves for access to grazing lands. The Herero proved able to press the Damara into subservience as their herdsmen. The largest of the groups, the Ovambo, also seemed the most inventive, early developing agricultural as well as blacksmith and woodworking skills. In the eighteenth century, a small group of Tswana moved into the easterly portion of the territory.

During the next century the expansion of the European colony at South Africa's Cape of Good Hope compelled several Nama groups to move back north across the Orange River, which led to intense conflict between them and the Herero. In addition, liaisons between Europeans and Nama in the Cape colony created a racially mixed Afrikaans-speaking community, the so-called Rehoboth Basters, who, having been expelled from the Cape, ultimately settled in an area south of present-day Windhoek. The Orlam, a group of Christian Nama, having access to European weapons, were often able to take over grazing lands previously occupied by the Herero, who had been drifting southward. By the time of the arrival of the Europeans in the nineteenth century, the Africans had developed a variety of social and political systems based on common ownership of the land and its resources—a tradition that would prove irreconcilable with that of the Europeans.

In 1850, after an extended series of contests, the Nama were able to gain the upper hand over the Herero and impose a temporary peace. A decade later, in fact, the Nama chief Jonker Afrikaner was in control of the bulk of the territory as far north as Ovamboland. A brilliant strategist, Afrikaner was described by the Swedish explorer Charles John Andersson as "the most industrious Hottentot" that he had ever seen.[2] Between 1860 and 1870, however, the

Herero, now gaining access to European arms, became successful in their "war of liberation" from Nama oppression and were able to make a dramatic, if short-lived, recovery under a succession of chiefs, including the dynamic Samuel Maharero. Subsequently, a second Nama dynasty renewed hostilities against the Herero. Its founder, Kupido Witbooi, was succeeded by his son and grandson, Moses and Hendrik Witbooi, the latter, "one of the most important historical figures in South West Africa."[3] Educated by Rhenish missionaries, he became chief of the Nama in 1887, firm in the belief that his rule was divinely appointed. His diary preserves one of the few black voices of his century for posterity.[4]

The Second Settlers

Namibian history began to involve Europeans on a continuing basis in 1805 with the arrival of representatives of the London Missionary Society (LMS). The first white settlers in the country were, however, two German brothers, Abraham and Christian Albrecht, sent by the LMS to initiate evangelistic work on what was hoped to be a self-supporting basis among two Nama tribes. They were joined in 1811 by the remarkable Johann Heinrich Schmelen and two other missionaries, including William Threlfall, who was murdered in 1825. Schmelen had first met a small group of Christian Nama while in London as a guest of the pastor of St. Mary's German Church there. His mission station in Namibia, Steinkopf, was named in honor of his pastor-friend back in London. Schmelen's identification with the Nama was total: electing to live as a Nama himself, he married a Nama.[5] One of the children of the union would become the wife of another missionary, Friedrich Kleinschmidt. Schmelen sufficiently mastered the Nama language to prepare a translation of the New Testament. His Schmelenhaus, erected at Bethany in 1814, is the oldest existing building of any type in the country. He even managed to develop rudimentary but invaluable roadways in the southern part of the territory. In 1842 the LMS and the Wesleyan Missionary Society, which had begun work in the Windhoek area, handed over responsibility for the Namibian field to the Rhenish Mission Society, in part because of the German support they had received.

The first missionaries sent by the Rhenish Society, Hugh Hahn and Friedrich Kleinschmidt, began their work with the Herero and Nama, respectively. Later the Damara would be included. More in jest than out of patriotic fervor, Hahn grandly called his little mission near Okahandji, "Gross Barmen." Kleinschmidt chose to name his station "Rehoboth," thus recalling the biblical Nimrod's Assyrian camp. Pietism's fondness for the nomenclature of biblical Israel had begun to color Namibian geography. The Austrian, Johan Rath, discovered springs at Otjimbingwe, and founded his mission station there—a site destined to serve briefly as the nation's capital, still a major center for the Namibian churches. While work among the Nama met with some success, Hahn and Rath could not make the same claim. A contemporary report observes:

> Year after year the word of God was sown among the Herero, but it appeared to fall on rock; it did not take root and was burned to death by the merciless sun. . . . What a meagre harvest it was when on the 25th of July 1858, the missionary Hahn at Barmen baptised his housemaid Uerieta. . . . And on the same day in Otjimbingwe, Rath baptized a man, Marcus, with his wife and child, six-year-old girl. That was the visible result after fourteen years of missionary work among the Herero.[6]

During this period Hahn and Rath had learned the Herero language sufficiently to compile a dictionary, a grammar, and readers, as well as to translate portions of the New Testament, all of which undergirded their regime of regularly preaching in the Herero language.

It would be a mistake to romanticize the beginnings of the Rhenish mission. Isolation, privation, and worse were constant. Letters from Europe could take two years to reach their destination. Frequent drought in an arid land often brought starvation in its wake. Schmelen, who had to clothe himself in skins, spoke of not having eaten bread for seven years. Hahn's wife and four children were lost in a shipwreck off Walvis Bay in 1859.

Particularly troubling, from the perspective of the mission, was the difficulty in defining an effective strategy. Some missionaries attempted to travel with the nomadic groups in an effort to develop an evangelistic ministry appropriate for pastoral life. Others sought to establish permanent stations where converts might settle. There an effort could be made to introduce farming in a land where it had been unknown. In addition, the establishment of trading centers, a direct attempt to circumvent the exploitation of the Africans by unprincipled traders, would also serve to make of the mission a key element in the new economic order. In time it became increasingly clear that only a settled ministry would prove viable, however revolutionary a challenge that would present to African tradition.

Some chiefs, not always interested in evangelization itself, but impressed by the ancillary benefits brought by the missions, were guardedly supportive of their work. Thus, on a trip north in 1866, Hugo Hahn was invited by two chiefs, Mweshipandeka Shaningika of Oukwanyama, and Shikongo Kalulu of Ondanga, to send missionaries into Ovamboland. Knowing that the Germans did not have resources to respond affirmatively, Hahn urged the Finnish Missionary Society (FMS) to do so. Eight Finnish missionaries arrived in 1870. Again the work proved arduous. Only after thirteen years did the FMS have its first six converts ready for baptism.

Particularly notable among the Finns was Martti Rautanen, "the apostle of Ovamboland," who, like the Germans to the south, was committed to literacy as a prime consideration. He reduced the Ndonga language into written form for use in his translations of the New Testament and a major portion of the Old. Six years after his arrival in the territory he was able to publish original materials: a primer and a collection of Bible stories.

Disease had severely afflicted the Ovambo before the arrival of the missionaries. Malaria was widespread; traditional taboos would not permit either handicapped children or twins to live. The Finnish response was to recruit professionally trained women in Europe. A medical doctor, Selma Raino, assisted by a corps of Finnish nurses, founded the Onandjokwe Hospital in 1908. Until the first male doctor arrived from Finland in 1952, professional medical care among the Ovambo was entirely in the hands of women. The importance of medical care from the perspective of the Ovambo people can hardly be overestimated. That this essential ministry was the responsibility of women, both Finnish and Ovambo, was eloquent testimony to the mission's belief in their competence.

The work of the Rhenish mission in the Oukwanyama area now divided by the Angola-Namibia border, was begun in 1891. Again, the major achievement initially lay not in rapid evangelization, but in creating the foundations for a literary culture: the Kwanyama language was mastered, readers were produced, and the New Testament was translated. When the Germans were forced to leave the area during World War I, nonordained Ovambo elders, equipped with the Scriptures and the beginnings of a literature in their own tongue, were pressed into leadership positions for the scattered flock. One innovation: the establishment of a series of "baptism schools" that prepared children and adults for entrance into the new faith. Earlier, in the central portion of the country, the establishment of mission stations proved providential during the wars between the Herero and Nama. As centers of succor and care for both groups, the missions slowly earned the confidence of the chiefs. During the so-called Second Herero-Nama War, it was even possible to establish new mission outposts. No apologist for the evangelization of Africa, Jon Manchip White has nonetheless given an appreciative assessment of the missionaries' work.

There is no doubt that, in many parts of the world, the missionary movements had an unfortunate influence on native peoples. Too often, instead of mitigating the harshness of imperial rule, they acted as its agents. They instilled a sense of sin and damnation that robbed many peoples of their confidence and energy, and by clumsy and ill-considered actions tore the whole fabric of tribal life apart. But it is only just to state that the sad pageant of history in South West Africa (Namibia) would have been far sadder had it not been for the intervention of the missionaries. Blessed, indeed, at that time were the missionaries. [They] . . . had to tread a thorny path. Their mission houses were burnt down around their ears. They were hounded and humiliated. Few groups of men have had such great need of faith, and few have ever shown so much of it.[7]

German Colonialism

Expansion as a permanent and supreme aim of politics is the central political idea of imperialism . . . an entirely new concept in the long history of political thought and action.
—Hannah Arendt, *The Origins of Totalitarianism*

To speak of Namibia as a part of a German Empire is, of course, an anachronism. The first Namibian experience with colonialism was, however, German. The oldest name for what is now Namibia was German South West Africa (Deutsch-Südwest-Afrika), in keeping with the common nineteenth-century notion that the globe generally is an appropriate theater for European expansion: economic, political, and religious. Politically, South West Africa lost its German connection with the invasion of British-led South African troops in 1915. Yet, seventy years later, the cultural legacy of imperial Germany is still unmistakably present. German remains one of the government's officially recognized languages. The capital city's main street, Kaiser Strasse, is crowned by the Wilhelmenian romanesque Christus Kirche (Christ Church). Children of all colors are given German names, particularly in southern Namibia. And since the political designs of successive imperialism, German, British, and South African, still hold the Namibian people in thrall, an examination of the territory's first experience with colonialism is basic for an understanding of its subsequent history.

A variety of actors animated by a diversity of intentions and reading from different scripts appear to wander off into political incoherence. From a distance a rough pattern can, however, be discerned. After a general settlement of the land by African peoples, Europeans enter with a bewildering and mutually contradictory agenda. Missionaries intent on evangelization press for literacy. Soon thereafter traders arrive seeking, of course, commercial profit. Bibles, rifles, and whiskey are pressed on the older culture, and each quickly shows its power. An imperial government, reluctant to enter the territory, politically assists in the formation of an "independent" German Colonial Society to encourage colonization by German emigrants. Then, by accident or design, the empire finds it necessary to utilize the society as a means for protecting the emigrants and strengthening its own economic interests in the area.

Christian missionaries found themselves torn by conflicting loyalties. As good Germans they rejoiced in the introduction of a familiar regime of law and order in a land where it seemed neither was present. And yet, as evangelists concerned with the welfare of their people, they could not be altogether sanguine concerning the prospects for their converts' material future. The increasing number of emigrants in the territory could only signal a loss of land, then a decay of social integrity and political freedom for the original population. Perhaps a solution, however faulty, might be obtained if one could somehow find it possible to disregard all merely material consideration. Perhaps a dualistic interpretation of the Gospel, one that affirms the spirit at the expense of the physical, would enable the mission to avoid having to champion the rights of the Africans.

It seemed obvious to nineteenth-century Europeans that national prestige required colonial possessions. In the case of the Germans, Prince Otto von Bismarck found Africa particularly attractive. The commercial expansion of the fatherland required new markets and greater access to raw materials. The German mission in Namibia did not oppose this development. Friedrich Fabri, director of the Rhenish Mission Society in Barmen, was particularly interested in encouraging German emigration to Namibia. A German colonization of the territory would, he believed, complement the work of the mission among the African population. Could not two quite separate Christian communities reflecting two quite distinct cultures be natural allies?

The development of the German Colonial Society for South West

Africa (Deutsche Kolonialgesellschaft für Südwest-Afrika) was the instrument by which the Prussian prince hoped to achieve his purpose. Under the motto, Where Trade Is, There the Flag Will Soon Follow, Bismarck set about to acquire the territory. German industry would get raw materials from the colony; the colony would become a new market for German industry. Surplus German population would not need to emigrate to America and so be lost to the German nation; emigration to a colony would serve to strengthen the empire's interests. Bismarck was convinced that the development of a colonial system would not prove to be a burden for the homeland politically. Entrepreneurs would assume the financial risks; the government would serve merely in a supervisory capacity. It should not be necessary to establish a large military force nor a governmental bureaucracy in the territory; the private commercial sector could be encouraged to provide staff and resources for colonial development.

In early May 1883 the dreams began to materialize. An entrepreneur from Bremen, Adolf Luederitz, through the good offices of a Rhenish missionary at Bethany, was able to purchase the Angra Pequena harbor and the land surrounding it for five miles in all directions for one hundred pounds and two hundred rifles. The following year he was able to make an additional purchase of a twenty-mile-wide strip along the coastline south from Walvis Bay, past Angra Pequena, to the Orange River, the South African border. In April 1884 Prince von Bismarck placed the whole strip under the protection of the German Empire. The German protectorate had begun. It is worth noting that in 1868 the mission had asked the British to provide protection for them but they were refused. The British position was that their responsibility was restricted to the area immediately surrounding Walvis Bay.[8] In July 1884 the British made their recognition of German sovereignty official. In the interests of furthering amicable relations between Prussia and Great Britain, the latter "does not contest the German government's claim to protect its German subjects settled among indigenous chiefs in Angra Pequena."[9] By July of 1885 Luederitz had been able to purchase coastal land all the way north to the Kuenene River, the northern border of today's Namibia. Thus, with the exception of the British-held Walvis Bay, the whole coast was in German hands.

The colonial policy of the Germans proved not so very different from that of the British and the Boers in South Africa. Clearly, if Europeans were to settle lands inhabited by Africans, their tradition of a communal occupation of grazing lands could not be permitted to continue. Private ownership of land, presupposed in a European system, could not be successfully combined with traditional open grazing. The latter, therefore, would have to be terminated. In Namibia the solution to the problem was reached by the creation of "Treaties of Protection" between individual tribal chiefs (or captains, as they were usually called) and the representatives of the German emperor. The formal purpose of the treaties was to provide protection to the Africans from incursions by rival tribes. From the European perspective, moral justification for the occupation of the territory could be sought in the apparent need to settle tribal disputes that at times threatened the security of the Europeans now entering the territory. In practice, however, the lands were "legally" alienated from tribal control. Military action by government troops began the process by establishing a "Police Zone" that would be made available for white settlers. Thus, by 1903, out of a total area of 33.82 million acres, the Africans had only 12.72 million left. The other 21.1 million were already in the hands of the newcomers: white settlers, the colonial government, and international corporations. Actual settlement was relatively limited until after the turn of the century. In 1897 there were barely 1,000 Europeans in the land. Sixteen years later there were close to 15 times as many.

The mission was active in encouraging local chiefs to sign protection treaties with the representatives of the empire. Chief Jacobus Isaak of Berseba, Chief Manasse of Hoachanas, and Headman Wilhelm Christina of the Bondelswarts, plus other Nama and Chief Maharero of the Herero, all signed treaties of protection with the Germans. Only after military defeat in 1894 would Hendrik Witbooi and Swartboois consent to a similar treaty. Thus the imperial representatives were successful in quickly placing a major portion of the country, excluding Ovamboland in the north, under their control.

The German treaties of protection were to prove, however, to be an unstable basis for colonial policy. Bismarck had wanted to win the confidence of the Africans by means of the treaties so that the trading companies would not need extensive military support.[10] Initially, Bismarck's plan had seemed promising. The Colonial Society had been granted extensive commercial rights and would clearly strengthen the German presence in the territory. Unfortunately, the task that lay before it proved far too demanding for its limited resources.[11]

In September 1887 the Nama chief, Hendrik Witbooi, mounted a daring attack on the military camp at Otjimbingwe, forcing Heinrich Goering, the imperial commissioner (and father of the

marshal in Hitler's Third Reich) to flee to the British at Walvis Bay
for protection. The reaction in Germany was sharply critical of the
"excessive softness" of Bismarck's policies. Strong punitive action
was demanded. The analysis offered by the jurist H. Hesse is
illustrative of an influential point of view.

> The dispute concerning the possession of the soil is the essence of the
> decisive fight in South West Africa. It is not the abuses of individual
> traders nor of individual officials, but solely the growing knowledge of
> the natives that their land is being transferred at a steady growing rate to
> the whites, which is the cause of the bloody rebellion in our protecto-
> rate. The price of victory will and must be the unconditional and
> absolute power of Germans over the South West African soil. The
> question of who should be masters in this territory can not be solved by
> agreements, small gifts, and eloquent speeches, but only by means of
> blood and iron.[12]

While right-wing juridical opinion cannot be regarded as representative of the full range of debate, the cry for a policy of "blood
and iron" did serve to envision the costs that would lie ahead. Clear
options were present. The Germans could hold either that their
government's presence in South West Africa was merely to protect
German nationals who had already chosen to settle there, or that
Berlin must aggressively seek to gain control of land suitable for
mining and agriculture as a base for increased colonization and
economic development. The first option was clearly welcomed by
the mission and had attraction for some tribal chiefs. The second
option would throw the mission into profound internal contradiction and would ultimately evoke a militant response from most of
the African groups.

A major psychological difficulty with the first option was its
implicit subversion of the racism enshrined in the law, mores, and
religion of the time. Under the protection treaties, conflicts between whites and blacks were to be settled by judges representing
the legal traditions of both cultures. Colonists and their supporters
in Europe found this insufferable. Typical is a colonial editor's
comment.

> This state of affairs of being subject to judgment by native judges—
> degrading for the Germans—definitely must come to an end. In addition
> to that, it cannot be expected of the white assistant judges of the
> imperial court, especially of its president, an imperial official, to sit
> down at the same table with the evil-smelling blacks. Finally, the
> qualification of the natives for the office of judge is highly contested,

due to the fact that the common sense of the native lay judges differs far too much from ours, as numerous incidents prove.[13]

The European need to establish some sort of legal principle as a precedent for political action was well illustrated in the judgment of the jurist Hesse.

> The nature of sovereignty is described by the sentence, *quid est in territoria, etiam est de territorio* (whatsoever is in the territory is absolutely subject to the ruling state administration). This total subjection of the natives under the government of the empire has to be brought about in the course of the rearrangement of affairs in South West Africa, that is by abolishing all existing privileges (claimed by the blacks).[14]

Clearly, it would be the second option that public opinion would increasingly demand as imperial policy.

The alienation of the great bulk of the territory from control of the indigenous people was achieved by a variety of methods. The signing of the so-called protection treaties between imperial representatives and tribal chiefs gave the Germans *de facto* recognition as the senior member of all such treaties. The uninhabited "no man's land" between the Ovambo and Herero people was simply declared crown property, there being no one there to object. Outright purchase or lease of valuable tracts at prices (in gold and guns) of extremely modest rates was more typical.

African reaction to aggressive colonialism was not difficult to anticipate. In 1887 a Herero group under the leadership of Chief Nicodemus was the first to rebel. Shortly afterward two Nama clans, the Afrikaner and the Swartbooi, also revolted. In late 1897 other Herero joined the rebellion. The last to oppose the Germans were the chiefs of Bethany and Warmbad. The imperial forces were able in each case to subdue their opponents. But a new, tougher policy clearly had to be devised. The most fateful proposal: the establishment of native reserves or "homelands," restricted areas in remote portions of the territory to which each tribal group could be legally assigned on a segregated tribal basis. This was not really new. Had not South African and North American precedents been established?[15]

One of the most outspoken, but, unfortunately, not unrepresentative, of the racists was Paul Rohrbach, who argued in his book *Deutsche Kolonialwirschaft* that the basic problem in the colonization of Africa lay in what he regarded as "the problem of the inferior race" *(der niederen Rasse)*. The black race was a people who had been, and always would be, inferior to the white race, the latter who had therefore earned the moral right to reign over them. The Boers of South Africa had shown the way forward: the land under question should be taken by "the better, the stronger race." Accordingly, all African structures should be terminated, the blacks permanently disarmed and trained as members of a servant class. The blacks have no right to the land merely because of earlier residence; only a people that is prepared to develop the territory has a legitimate claim to ownership. Ultimately, all of subtropical Africa should be, for moral and rational reasons, opened up for settlement by the whites. Concern for the human rights of African peoples is misplaced, since as savages they fall outside the moral traditions of Western civilization. With respect to South West Africa, the goal of colonialism is the extension of German nationhood within which there is no place for the retention of an uncivilized society.[16]

On another occasion Rohrbach went on to argue on behalf of the colonists at Windhoek.

> The decision to colonize South West Africa means nothing less than that the native tribes must withdraw from the lands on which they have pastured their cattle and so let the white man pasture his cattle on the selfsame lands. If the moral right of this standpoint is questioned, the answer is that for people of the cultural standard of the natives, the loss of their free national barbarism and the development of a class of workers in the service of and dependent on the whites is primarily a law of existence in the highest degree. . . . For a people, as for an individual, an existence appears to be justified in the degree that it is useful in the progress of general development. By no argument in the world can it be shown that the preservation of any degree of national independence, national prosperity, and political organization by the races of South West Africa would be of greater or even equal advantage for the development of mankind in general or the German people in particular than that these races should be made serviceable in the enjoyment of their former territories by the white races.[17]

Conflict between the missionaries and other Germans in the territory often centered in their divergent attitudes toward the Africans. One missionary reported that

> [t]he real cause of the bitterness among the Herero toward the Germans is without question the fact that the average German looks down upon the natives as being about on the same level as the higher primates, baboon being their favorite term for the natives, and treats them like animals. The settler holds that the native has a right to exist in so far as

he is useful to the white man. It follows that the whites value their horses and even their oxen more than they value the natives.[18]

That the mission itself could not be considered free from contemporary racism is displayed in the work of F. Fabri, head of the Rhenish Mission Society, who eagerly embraced the biblical interpretation commonly taught by the Boers of South Africa: the divine curse placed on Cain in Genesis 4 requires forever a subordinate destiny for all people of color.[19]

In the late 1880s gold was discovered near the Rhenish mission at Otjimbingwe. The dramatic increase in white adventurers alarmed the local Herero chief, Kamaherero, who had become increasingly suspicious of all whites, including the mission staff. Further disenchantment sprang from the failure of the imperial forces to keep the promises defined in the protection treaties. The major challenge to the German military would come, however, from the Nama under the charismatic leadership of Hendrik Witbooi. The imperial staff had concluded that the unyielding resistance of Witbooi to German rule could not be tolerated indefinitely. The first major encounter took place on 12 April 1893 with the severe defeat of the Nama forces. The report of Inspector Schreiber to the Rhenish Mission Society four months later is revealing.

> Hendrik Witbooi's fortress . . . was conquered by the [German] protective force at the beginning of April. Unfortunately women and children have been killed. Hendrik himself has escaped and will probably cause further trouble for the Germans. He is extremely bitter against them and claims that he could not at all understand why he, such a peace loving man, had been attacked without any reason. . . . This vigorous proceeding of the Germans has obviously impressed the whole country tremendously, and it may be hoped that the Herero too will now submit to German sovereignty at all events. On the other hand, it is to be desired that their rights should be respected as much as possible and that they are led to regard the German government as a blessing for the country.[20]

Schreiber's narrative exposes contradictory convictions jostling for dominance. Determined to punish the Herero for reputed atrocities inflicted by them on the Nama, Witbooi was determined to overpower the Nama's enemies once and for all. A devout Christian, Witbooi believed that he had been called by God to punish the Herero for their wickedness. But what was more significant, as he indicated in his diary, was his conviction that God the Creator had given this land to the Africans. It was this belief that provided a moral basis for his struggle. The coming of the Europeans as a colonial power was contrary to the will of God and must be opposed in God's name. Thus, those Africans who support the German occupation (such as the Herero) are disloyal both to their tribal heritage and to the divine will.

The German foreign office was not particularly sympathetic to Witbooi's argument or objective. Continued conflict between tribal groups had suggested that the protection treaties were worthless. That an imperial force could not impose law and order on ill equipped, illiterate Africans had become a humiliation that could no longer be tolerated.

Caught between Witbooi and the imperial government, the mission chose, with little apparent difficulty, to support the policy of the fatherland. Fearing Witbooi's influence in the church, the mission obtained his removal as an elder in the congregation—the highest rank open to an African in the church at that time. With Witbooi removed it believed that the imposition of German military force could bring an end to the traditional conflict between the Herero and the Nama. Witbooi's desire to be the dominant political force in the country would never win the assent of the Herero or other tribes, whatever position the German foreign office might take.

Born in 1838, Hendrik Witbooi had been converted to Christianity as a young man through the work of the Rhenish mission. It also provided him with a basic education. Biblical history had made a particularly strong impression on Witbooi, who began to see himself as called to be a leader of the Nama similar to the judges of Israel during their conquest of Canaan. He saw himself as a servant of the Lord called to punish the Nama's old foes, the Herero, whom he regarded as the new Canaanites. On a visit in Hereroland in 1880, his group was attacked by a Herero raiding party, he alone of the Nama surviving. He regarded his escape as a miracle. On his way home he had a vision in which he saw himself anointed to be the leader of all the Nama. In their conflict with the Herero, the victory of the Nama would make possible an entry into a promised land, a recapitulation of Israel's conquest of Canaan. His first incursion into Hereroland proved to be a brilliant success, resulting in a treaty that gave some of the Herero's land to the Nama and permitting Witbooi to travel at will through the territory. Firmly believing in the sanctity of his call to serve his people, Witbooi did not hesitate to proclaim himself *summus episcopus* (supreme bishop) when the Rhenish mission closed its station in his area. The contemporary assessment of the local *Deutsche Kolonialzeitung* was accurate. The Nama "believe in his mission and his vision and follow him."[21]

Witbooi distinguished sharply between the mission and the German community generally. His assessment of the German military in a colonial court is telling: the German, he wrote,

> [m]akes no quest according to truth and justice and asks no permission of a chief. He introduces laws into the land [which] are entirely impossible, untenable, unbelievable, unbearable, unmerciful and unfeeling. . . . He personally punishes our people at Windhoek and has already beaten people to death for debts. . . . It is not just and right to beat people to death for that. . . . He flogs people in a shameful and cruel manner. We are stupid and unintelligent people (for so he thinks us to be), yet we have never yet punished a human being in such a cruel and improper way. He stretches people on their backs and flogs them on the stomach and even between the legs, be they male or female, so your honor can understand that no one can survive such a punishment.[22]

Hendrik Witbooi, alone of all the chiefs in the main body of the territory, refused to accept the German claim to sovereignty. His religious-political vision, however persuasive for his followers, raised an intolerable obstacle to European plans for the territory. In an attempt to bring him under control, the German captain, Curt von Francois, requested and got 250 additional troops from Germany. Attacking Witbooi's camp without warning, they were able to kill 150 Nama, including 78 women and children. The imperial troops had demonstrated their power, but proved unable to capture Witbooi himself, who subsequently requested von Francois to send him ammunition to replenish the Nama's supplies, arguing that only if both sides had weapons could von Francois's victory be considered an honorable one!

In Germany the *Reichstag* responded in dismay at the news of von Francois's draconian methods. He was replaced by Major Theodor Leutwein in January 1894 with clear orders to pacify, not annihilate, the local population.[23] But even Leutwein was compelled to wait for further reinforcements from Germany before he could finally defeat Witbooi's army.

Within eight months of his arrival in the territory, Leutwein had been able both to win the general support of the Herero, who regarded the Nama under Witbooi as their major enemy, and to extract a peace treaty from Witbooi. Leutwein's liberal provisions permitted the Nama to retain their horses, guns, and lands in exchange for a promise to assist the Germans militarily, in fact, to be their ally "in any future wars." Leutwein thus brilliantly demonstrated his mastery of the policy of *divide et impera:* the major African tribes had come to regard each other as their primary opponent, with the Germans as their primary ally. Leutwein, playing on the intertribal suspicions, was able to establish clear German hegemony throughout the bulk of the protectorate.

The Rhenish mission believed that only German sovereignty could bring peace and security to the land. Witbooi, of course, was even more convinced of the truth of his own vision. When the mission saw that he would prove intractable, it resorted to an extraordinary act of censure: refusal of the sacrament. Witbooi accepted his excommunication with equanimity. He continued to regard the missionaries as servants of God and would not permit his associates to speak against them. Nonetheless, the assessment of Loth is just.

> The fight carried on by Hendrik Witbooi for the unity and independence of the tribes under a religious flag ended with a temporary defeat of the "heretic" and with a triumph of the Rhenish mission and its ideology and mission policy, both serving colonialism.[24]

Witbooi remained at peace with the Germans for a decade. Then, in the uprising of 1904–7 he joined forces with his old enemies, the Herero, to fight again for the freedom of his land.

Witbooi is the most interesting figure in nineteenth-century Namibian history. What in a later time would be called a theology of liberation, was anticipated by him and became the measure of his religious commitment. Basically, he was an exemplar of the fruitfulness of the pietist faith.[25] His pastors' emphasis on Bible study and personal religious experience had proven to be in Southern Africa no mere reaction against a European state church religion. Transplanted by missionaries, it could take root in an exotic world, there to flourish and grow. Witbooi was a particularly striking instance of its potentiality. Using the literacy gained at the mission he was able not only to read the Bible "for himself"; he could come to understand his vocation under God to be the liberation for his own people. In his study of the Old Testament he was profoundly moved by the narratives disclosing the divine intention of freedom for Israel. As the Hebrew people fought the Canaanites with the blessing of God, could not the Nama look to victory over their Herero opponents? Was not Israel's story of salvation the very antitype of his people's bondage to another powerful empire? Reading the Bible "for himself," Witbooi could find in its narrative no precedent for colonialism: the entrance of the imperialist forces into Namibia was clearly contrary to the message of holy writ! The increasingly violent penetration of the whites into Southern Africa is an open defiance of God's will. Yet God would still work on his salvation through the history of the land, even if the mission had proven more loyal to the imperial army than to its African congregations.

Throughout the wars, Witbooi held services of Christian worship in his camp, himself presiding. When removed from his position of leadership in the mission, he founded his own parish, an independent congregation at Hoornkranz, not so much out of a desire to be schismatic, but rather to assure that his understanding of the message of the Bible for Africa, and his own experience of the power of that Word, would not be silenced.

Clearly, the declaration of the protectorate had not brought peace to the territory. And while tensions between tribes continued, the thrust of the conflict increasingly shifted to hostilities between African and imperial forces. Berlin's unwillingness to commit more than token forces to the struggle enraged the colonists, and dismayed the political right at home. The only solution acceptable to both groups was one that would lead to success, i.e., the unqualified subjugation of Africans to German authority. But the only method by which that could be achieved would call for a massive escalation in military pressure. The increasing popularity of a military solution was an admission of failure for what had been imperial policy: the German colonial presence in the territory had proven unacceptable to the African population after all. Berlin could argue that the failure of "the savages" to appreciate the superior qualities of European civilization was evidence of the inadequacy of any moral claim that might be offered in their defense. Clearly, the colony could have no future promise as long as the original inhabitants could successfully challenge the authority of newcomers. The Africans' resistance would have to be broken if the Europeans were to live in peace. Such defenders of tribal power as Witbooi would have to be brought to their knees. In Germany and among the colonists, popular opinion increasingly demanded an armed subjugation of the Africans.

Between 1893 and the 1904-7 war, the tensions between the imperial and African forces were never resolved. The Bondelswart rebellion of 1903, mounted by the Swartbooi Nama, was a prelude to later devastation. Initially the Nama were able to expose the weakness of the European troops. Unable to master the situation, Leutwein was forced to sue for a temporary peace. Subsequently, the Germans were able to renew their attack, claim the victory, and lay heavy penalties. In addition to surrendering all arms, the defeated were required to pay for all costs sustained by the imperial troops by ceding to the Germans still more Swartbooi land.

Genocide

The German-Namibian war of 1904–7 was to prove an unmitigated disaster. For the Herero and the Nama, the struggle would be no "mere incident, but rather the greatest historical event which [they had] ever experienced. It was their Marathon, their Cannae, their Sedan, their Hiroshima,"[26] contends the historian, Jon M. Bridgman. He continues, "The total dead was probably greater than in the Boer War, the Crimean War, the Spanish American War, the Seven Weeks War and in a dozen or more other conflicts that were fought between 1815 and 1917."[27] The mind strains—unable to grasp the enormity of the slaughter. Largely ignored by standard histories of European colonialism, the war remains as an appalling demonstration of the power of public opinion to demand, with close to complete success, that a defeated people be annihilated.

The transformation of the Herero people within a generation of contact with the German colonists had been a dramatic chapter in Namibian history. The basic differentiations of a class structure had their beginnings in Herero tribal life.[28] A class of affluent cattle owners, possessing up to ten thousand head of cattle, sheep, and goats, contrasted with the less prosperous who had few or no animals of their own. Each of the Herero tribes was headed by a chief who ruled by right of inheritance. All land, of course, was held in common by the tribe and could not be alienated, except in rare cases. But by the time of the beginning of the German protectorate, this traditional pattern had already begun to change. The Herero, no longer free to move over tribal lands at will, were under increasing pressure to establish permanent settlements and to move into a money economy. The basic wealth, cattle, could be sold for European goods. It proving difficult to deal with the loose association of tribal groups, the Germans selected a particular chief, Samuel Maharero, to serve as paramount chief of all Herero, although such centralization of tribal power had previously been unknown. Maharero, a Christian, symbolized the transformation of African culture into one of accommodation to the European presence.[29]

The German protectorate, for all of its stress on security and order, never proved able to achieve its public purpose, the establish-

Survivors of the German-Namibian War. *(Courtesy of IDAF.)*

ment of civil peace in the territory. Its first decade was marked by successive outbreaks of warfare between the indigenous tribes and the European authorities. As we have seen, the Bondelswart revolt of 1903 was quashed only with the greatest difficulty. The next four years saw most of central and south Namibia in a continual state of rebellion. The focus of the conflict lay between the imperial forces on the one hand, and the former rival tribes, the Herero and Nama, on the other. Before the struggle would come to its end, the European forces under General Lothar von Trotha would raise the curtain on the twentieth-century's experiments in genocide: tens of thousands of men, women, and children would see death in open warfare, in concentration camps, and, worst of all, in desert exile.

The literature describing the causes of the conflict is remarkably straightforward. Technically, the 1904–7 war was a conflict over land. With the establishment of the protectorate in 1884, it had become increasingly clear that whatever its theoretical intent, its actual consequence was the removal of tribal groups from their traditional territory. The choice seemed simple. Is the land to be controlled by its indigenous population for their benefit, or is it to be incorporated into an imperial system for the primary use of the European community? Compromise seemed unthinkable. Imperial policy would have but two objectives: South West Africa would be a "model European territorial state," an extension of the fatherland, governed by German laws and inhabited by German citizens. The new state would replace traditional tribal political structures. The role of the blacks when in contact with the whites would be that of a servant class.

With the introduction of the German protectorate, the Herero, in particular, saw the alienation of much of their best land and cattle into the hands of the colonialists. In order to obtain the traders' merchandise, the African would be obliged to sell his livestock. In a contemporary account, a German officer describes how the process would work.

> The Herero brings the oxen which he wishes to sell. "How much do you want for the oxen?" says the trader. "Fifty pounds sterling," replies the Herero. "Good," says the trader. "Here you have a coat valued at twenty pounds, trousers worth ten pounds, and coffee and tobacco worth twenty pounds. This is all fifty pounds." The Herero is satisfied; he knows that according to the custom of the traders he cannot expect more for his cattle. He may probably exchange the coat for a blanket and get some sugar *in lieu* of tobacco, and he will also, by begging, get a little extra. If, however, he does not succeed, the transaction is closed. It will be admitted that this sort of trading is exceptional and quite original. It requires to be learned and the newcomer will have to pay for his experience before he is able to emulate the dodges and tricks of the old traders.[30]

Perhaps the most dangerous aspect of this method of exchange was the introduction of extending credit. The traders would give the Africans the desired goods with nothing down, on the promise of future payment. At the time of payment, high interest rates could result in a debt many times greater than the value of the original purchase—an innovation quite novel to the African.

Far more serious than the loss of cattle, which in time could be remedied, was the loss of land. By 1904, the Africans had only 12.72 million acres left, while the Europeans had 21.1. It had become clear to the chiefs that the rapid alienation of the land, if permitted to continue unchecked, would leave the tribes without a viable future.

On the other hand, it had seemed to the colonists that the German government had not moved with sufficient decisiveness in subduing the "rebellious" tribes. The intermittent wars among the tribes threatened the security of the colonists who looked to Berlin to provide a military solution. In Germany too, the dominant sentiment pressed for a speedy subjugation of the Africans. Particularly galling was the stubborn resistance of the Nama chief, Hendrik Witbooi, who was seen by the Germans as their premier African opponent. If there were to be a secure future for the whites in the protectorate, it seemed clear that the Nama would have to be defeated.

Typical of the colonialist justification of the need to take to arms were the views of Herr Pfeil, a leader of the Windhoek community.

Whereas in the economic and political as well as the administrative fields we rather uncertainly felt our way, we behaved with much self assurance as soon as our feelings were based on military engagements. These feelings could not have been aroused more appropriately than by our fellow countrymen being murdered by a horde of wild tribes, whose most brutal instincts had been unchained. Without any doubt, one may admit that the Herero are a nation of lords, whereas this quality must be denied the Hottentots [Nama]. But even though they are a *Herrenvolk* [masterful people], they are still wild, unable to see common humanity in the enemy.[31]

Casual morality is not, of course, unusual in a frontier town. So Pfeil could argue that

[e]ven if irregularities in our conduct of the war have occurred, and even if such faults have been committed now and then, which war is free of such? They can have little weight, when the action taken has, on the whole, brought about success. And we look back on quite a bit of success in our warfare against the natives. The tribes are scattered. Their power is broken. We control the situation, and it can hardly be assumed that the tribes would be able to rise against us right away should we suddenly cease our military operations.[32]

The relative security of Windhoek during the conflict seems to have encouraged support for policies that would lead to speedy success in the conduct of the war. Major Theodor Leutwein, commander of the German forces, was subject to criticism in the territory as well as in Germany for not being more decisive. Colonial advocates of a Herrenmenschenpolitik ("policy of superiority") urged vigorous military action. Their opponents, missionaries, "idealists," and various Humanitaetsduselei ("humanitarian fools") were dismissed as not being sufficiently appreciative of the need for vigorous military action to establish unequivocally German supremacy in the territory. A particularly revealing episode illustrating the quality of colonial justice and suggesting the rationale for Herero resentment has been preserved in Leutwein's memoirs.

In the early part of 1903 an intoxicated white man shot a Herero woman, who was sleeping peacefully in a wagon. He did this because he thought he was being attacked and so he fired blindly in all directions. The court rejected the contention that he was actually being attacked, so the case turned on the questions of the hallucinations of a drunkard. The judges found the man not guilty because they accepted the defense that he had acted in good faith. This acquittal aroused extraordinary excitement in Hereroland, especially since the murdered woman was the daughter of a chief. Everywhere the question was asked: "Have the white people the right to shoot native women?" I traveled to Hereroland to pacify the people as far as I was able and also to make clear to them that I did not agree with the judgment of the court, but that I had no influence over it. Luckily the prosecutor appealed. The accused was then brought before the Supreme Court in Windhoek and sentenced to three years imprisonment. The event, however, had contributed its share toward the unrest among the Herero which resulted in the outbreak of their rebellion a half year later.[33]

In a confidential report to the Colonial Office in Berlin, Leutwein provided fuller information that is rather more incriminating: the accused was a tradesman named Dietrich who, while walking to the town of Omaruru, was overtaken by a wagon driven by the son of a Herero chief accompanied by his wife and child. Dietrich was offered a ride. During the night the Herero heard screams and a shot. He found his wife dead, having been shot when she resisted Dietrich's attempt at rape. After the outbreak of the Herero war, Dietrich's sentence was lifted and he was made a noncommissioned officer in the volunteers.

Traditionally dominant in the central portion of the country, the Herero were the first to feel the consequences of the settling of the land by German farmers and ranchers. As long as the tribes could move freely with their cattle, an essential requirement in so arid a climate, the Africans argued there was no insurmountable difficulty to prevent the coexistence of traditional and European economies. But as the best and largest portions of the land came under white control, the Herero became increasingly aware of their tenuous future. Their major advocate, both in Germany and Namibia, was the Rhenish mission. Unfortunately, however, the mission vacillated among alternative policies and thus undercut its own potential effectiveness. Some in the mission protested the government's policy of purchasing land for resale to the settlers. Since the mission stations had initially been established in the better areas, there was danger that they would end up being surrounded by European colonists. Other mission leaders were less critical of the German government, the political authority to which they felt they owed primary loyalty. Religiously inclined to regard such worldly matters as land ownership as beyond their responsibility or competence, they failed to recognize that their support of imperial policy could only serve to send mixed signals to their congregations. The mission that was publicly committed to evangelization of the Namibian people supported, in practice, a foreign government that denied the Namibians control of their traditional lands.

From the perspective of military history, it is not the final defeat of the Herero and Nama, but the long denial of victory to the Germans, that is more surprising. The most powerful military machine in the world, using weaponry created by early twentieth-century technology, was held at bay for three years by apparently disorganized Africans armed with little more than rifles obtained by barter from European colonists. The Germans were vastly superior to the Africans in arms and numbers. All that distinguished the Africans in the defense of their homeland was the conviction that it was their cause that was morally right. They believed that appeal to either African or Christian morality would justify their case. In addition, the Africans possessed a superior knowledge of the terrain, which gave them a tactical advantage and an ease of mobility that the Germans could not match. In time, the invaders would win, but only at the cost of a protracted humiliation at the hands of supposedly "inferior, half savage natives."

Early 1904 witnessed one disaster after another for the imperial troops. The general staff in Berlin concurred that Leutwein would have to be replaced by a more aggressive, more experienced leader. General Lothar von Trotha, seasoned in the German East African campaign of a decade earlier, was chosen. He would later reveal his understanding of his new charge.

> His majesty, the emperor and king, said to me that he expected that I would crush the uprising with any means necessary and only then inform him of the reasons for the uprising.[34]

Confiding to Leutwein the need for a drastic change in policy, von Trotha explained:

> I know the tribes of Africa. They are all alike. They only respond to force. It was and is my policy to use force with terrorism and even brutality. I shall annihilate the revolting tribes with streams of blood and streams of gold. Only after a complete uprooting will something emerge.[35]

In June, fearing that the ruthlessness of the general's policy would destroy the colony's priceless asset—its population, Leutwein proposed to von Trotha that the Herero be offered amnesty in exchange for surrendering their arms. Von Trotha, however, remained adamant, and Leutwein was subsequently confined to largely civilian administrative duties.

The decisive contest came at the Battle of Waterberg in August. Von Trotha had close to 5,000 men (an army that would later reach 20,000). Under the leadership of chief Samuel Maharero, some 6,000 Herero, defending 40,000 women and children, were encamped south of the Waterberg. Maharero was confident of victory, largely because of the difficulty he knew the Germans would encounter in having to cross some 100 miles of semidesert. But by 11 August, von Trotha's forces, supported by 3 machine gun sections and 32 artillery pieces, had compressed the large Herero body into a 5- by 10-mile rectangle. Panic broke out in the Herero camp as German artillery exacted its heavy toll. Von Trotha shrewdly permitted the Herero to "escape" southeast—into the desert from which few would return.

> Upon receiving news of the Herero rout, the emperor wired von Trotha: With thanks to God and with great joy I have received your report from Hamakari concerning the successful attack of August 11 against the main force of the Herero. Though the heavy losses suffered because of the enemy are to be regretted, yet the bravery which the troops displayed under the greatest tension and deprivation . . . fill me with pride. I give you, your officers and men, my imperial thanks and fullest recognition of what you have done. William.[36]

The realities in the field provided a somewhat different perspective. One officer, in command of a unit of African troops (a small group of Basters, Witboois, and Bethany Coloreds), later testified under oath:

> When the fight was over, we discovered eight or nine sick Herero women who had been left behind. Some of them were blind. They had no water and food. The German soldiers burned them alive in the huts in which they lay.[37]

Having turned seventy Herero prisoners of war over to the Germans, the same officer discovered two days later they had all been killed. A Damara leader and ally of the Germans also testified under oath:

> We hesitate to kill Herero women and children, but the Germans spared no one. They killed thousands and thousands. I saw this slaughter for day after day.[38]

Waterberg was not the end of the war, but it marked the inevitable defeat of the Herero. Von Trotha could truly write, "All contacts with the enemy since the battle of Waterberg have demonstrated that their strength of will, unity of command, and last remnants of resistance have been lost."[39] Most of the surviving Herero had been driven into the desert wastes. German patrols later reported finding the wilderness littered with hundreds of bodies. Dry holes as deep as forty feet had been dug by the Herero in a futile attempt to find water.

In a final attempt to bring hostilities to a swift conclusion, von Trotha announced on 2 October his final solution to the Herero problem.

I, the great general of the German troops, send this letter to the Herero people. The Herero are no longer German subjects. They have murdered and stolen; they have cut off the noses, ears, and other bodily parts of wounded soldiers. And now, because of cowardice, they will fight no more. I say to this people: Any one who delivers one of the Herero captains to my station as a prisoner will receive 1,000 marks. He who brings in Samuel Maharero will receive 5,000 marks. All the Herero must leave the land. If the people do not do this, I will force them to do it with the great guns. Any Herero found within the German borders with or without a gun, with or without cattle, will be shot. I shall no longer receive any women or children. I will drive them back to their people or I will shoot them. This is my decision for the Herero people.

The Great General of the Mighty Emperor, von Trotha.[40]

In late December the emperor, under urging of the chancellor, Buelow, reluctantly agreed to suspend von Trotha's declaration. In the future, any Herero who surrendered would not be summarily killed, but would be chained, pressed into service as a forced laborer, and branded with the letters GH (Gefangene Herero ("captured Herero"). However, Herero, who refused to disclose the location of their weapons caches, would be shot. The policy was effective. By September 1905 only a few dozen Herero remained in the old Hereroland. In April of 1905 von Trotha moved to suppress the Nama as decisively as he had defeated the Herero. At Gibeon he called for their immediate surrender.

The mighty and powerful German emperor will grant mercy to the Hottentot [Nama] people and will spare the lives of those who voluntarily surrender. . . . Those who do not submit will suffer the same fate that befell the Herero, who in their blindness believed they could carry on a successful war with the mighty German emperor and the great

German people. I ask you, where are all the Herero today, where are their chiefs? . . . The Hottentots will suffer the same fate if they do not surrender and give up their weapons . . . . He who believes that mercy will not be extended to him should leave the land, for as long as he lives on German soil he will be shot. This policy will be maintained until all such Hottentots have been killed.[41]

At the outbreak of the war the Herero had numbered 80,000. In 1911 only 15,130 had survived in South West Africa. A few had escaped east into British territory, modern Botswana. Many had died in concentration camps while "German patrols hunted down [the remaining Herero] like wild beasts all during 1905."[42]

In late October, the Nama chief, Hendrik Witbooi, was mortally wounded and succeeded by his son, Isaak. However, actual power fell into the hands of the head of a peace party, Chief Samuel Isaak, who sued for the cessation of hostilities the following month. Early the next year the last major resistance of the Nama had ended, although sparodic uprisings continued. It was not until the end of March 1907, however, that the Germans could finally declare the territory pacified.

In the end the Herero and the Nama would never know their traditional life again. But the German claim to exemplify the moral superiority of a civilized nation had also been lost. The Germans have never maintained that their defeat of the Africans was a moral victory. Ironically, only eight years later the Germans would lose the colony in yet another war. Has ever a victor demanded so much to achieve so little?

The losses sustained by the Nama were statistically less than the Herero's but no less horrifying. In 1904 there had been some 20,000 Nama; 7 years later the number had been reduced to 9,781. Again, all deaths were not on the field of battle. Out of a group of 1,800 exiled to an island camp, only 245 had survived by April 1907. And of that number, only 25 were strong enough to work. In sum, the Herero were reduced to 19 percent of their previous number, the Nama to 49 percent. Decimation is, of course, far too weak a word to describe such losses. Holocaust, we have been rightly reminded, should not be used to describe a massacre less severe than that suffered by the Jewish people during the Nazi period, when one third of world Jewry was destroyed. In Namibia early in the twentieth century, however, 81 percent of the Herero and 51 percent of the Nama were annihilated and no one thought to whisper, holocaust. No less incredible, surely, is this: the academic community, the political fora, the mass media, and the churches, seem to have agreed. It is permissible to forget Namibia's genocide.

2
Missions, Churches, and Politics

Religion is the substance of culture, culture is the expression of
religion.
—Paul Tillich, *The Protestant Era*

Religion and Law in African Tradition

It has been characteristic for African religion to serve as an organic
part of the social structure, essential for its stability and cohesion.
Recurring similarities in cultic practice and tribal life have been
discovered by anthropologists throughout sub-Saharan Africa.
Thus, belief in a creator God, often styled "the Oldest" or "the
High God," has been common.[1] Stories about him employ a variety
of names, but he is typically pictured as having withdrawn from
contact with human society in the primoridal past to dwell in the
heavens, far from the world of ordinary people.[2] Among some of
the northern tribes of Namibia, he was known as Kalunga and was
regarded as both omnipresent and omniscient: he was not seen but
could see all. He was beyond good and evil, but was the ultimate
source of both.[3] Life and rain, death and pestilence all came from
him. He was not subject to barter and thus was too exalted to be
affected by human disrespect and irreverence. Significantly, however, he was related, not primarily to the individual who had but
little conscious reality, but to society as the fundamental human
unit. While Kalunga was not the author of societal customs or
moral obligations, he was seen as their guarantor demanding conformity with them. Thus, a violation of the ethnic code was not a sin
against Kalunga as such, but rather an affront to the community
and its ancestral spirits. He stood as the ultimate sanction for
community conformity to tribal tradition. Reverence for the spirits
of the tribe's ancestors was particularly important, for they were the
agents of continuity between the present and the past, essential
instruments for tribal solidarity. The future, conceived as a projec-
tion of lineal time from the past through the present, had little
reality.

With the coming of the missionaries, the message of the God of the Bible, also called Kalunga, served both to affirm and to challenge traditional beliefs. Reverence for the spirits of the ancestors as mediators of supernatural power would diminish as the power and presence of the God of the Bible were proclaimed. The remoteness of the deity was overcome. The primacy of the tribe as the fundamental social unit found resonance and reinforcement in the biblical emphasis on the solidarity of the community. The social novelty in the missionary' message lay in its preoccupation with the salvation of the individual, an astonishing innovation from the African perspective. The belief that each person is unique in the eyes of God—quite apart from traditional social ties—would work a psychological revolution, transforming the traditional culture irrevocably. In Namibia the discovery of the spiritual dignity of the individual exposed a dimension of the human spirit that had previously lain dormant. Significantly, this awareness was not understood to require an abandonment of the inherent sense of corporate identity. The individualism of nineteenth-century piety asserted by the missions could not dissolve the social consciousness of African culture. A distinctive African Christianity, saved from the one-sided, frequently introverted biases of European piety, could now evolve.

If the Europeans did not bring belief in God to Africa, it is also clear that they did not bring the concept of political authority either. The common assumption among nineteenth-century Europeans that the African people were "uncivilized" because, among other things, they lacked a legal tradition resting on a tested political structure, was fundamentally mistaken. In spite of the general disdain for African culture common during the colonial era, some missionaries found it possible to come to a much more positive assessment of the African understanding of law and order.

Early in the century, the Rhenish missionary, C. Wandres, published a significant study of the legal traditions of the Nama and Damara, showing that the structures of civil law were effectively preserved in the oral tradition of the community, consensus on the basis of tradition providing the normative principle.[4] Prohibitions were clear. Murder, theft, disobedience to elders, and adultery, were punished, giving striking confirmation to the missionaries' Lutheran belief in a divine law, roughly similar to the Ten Commandments, written on all human hearts. Elaborate procedures governing jury trial had been developed. Judges could serve both as defense counsel and as prosecutor in minor cases. Ordinarily, the elders of the tribe would be chosen to serve as officers of the court.

In the case of a serious offense, several judges would participate, one serving as defense counsel for the accused. Typically, witnesses to the offense would be required, preferably an eyewitness. Witnesses could be cross-examined by anyone present at the trial. If the contesting parties could not reach an agreement in spite of the judge's efforts, then a duel, without weapons, could be prescribed. The victor would, however, be required to give a feast as a sign of reconciliation, featuring the opponents eating from a common bowl.

Taking the law into one's hands to collect debts was unknown, as was trial by ordeal or the swearing of oaths. Elaborate regulations were also established for criminal law and property ownership. Capital punishment could be decreed for murder, repeated theft, treason, and incest. Abortion was punishable by forty lashes; if the woman died, the abortionist received the death penalty. The common ownership of hunting and pasture land simplified property regulations. Herds were not owned by the tribe, and were considered to be the main body of family wealth. Slavery was unknown. Wealthy families might have servants who in some cases could marry into the family. Loans could be agreed upon verbally, but the charging of interest was unknown. A debtor who refused to make repayment could be prosecuted, as the breaking of a solemn promise to pay was regarded as particularly dishonorable. All material possessions were the property of the tribe or family. In a marriage, husbands and wives had no separate ownership. Upon the death of a husband, the wife and children were declared heirs and would receive equal shares.

It is clear that the Namibians, far from being "lawless savages," had evolved a strong legal tradition expressive of strong community solidarity. Specific rules varied among the tribes, but the seriousness with which a tribe's moral traditions was held was seen as a measure of the legitimacy of the authority of the chief. Western civilization did not bring the concept of justice or the practice of law to Namibia. It rather introduced new practices that partly affirmed, and partly contradicted, Namibian traditions. The later revolts against the colonial powers were, after all, only intelligible on the assumption that the tribal chiefs were obliged to defend, or reclaim, their ancient rights. The revolt of the Nama and the Herero, far from proving an African lawlessness, sprang from a dispute between two conflicting systems of legal authority. The European need to justify legally the occupation of the territory could only collide with the Africans' need to defend an immemorial patrimony, the loss of which would mean the end of their world.[5]

Pietism's Daughters

The role of the churches in this clash of cultures is particularly complex. While missionaries and traders had begun to explore Namibia early in the nineteenth century, the first major effort at evangelization was the work of the Rhenish Mission Society in 1842. In the words of the Oblate missionary priest, Heinz Hunke:

> The German missionaries who entered the country and attempted to establish Christianity among the different tribes were the initiators of a long history of personal dedication to a high spiritual ideal, belief in a religious mission, zeal for German Christian civilization, and denial of any proper value of African society, ethics, or religion. In Namibia, as in other parts of Africa, Christianization began when the dominating European ideology had already become a spiritualistic and individualist morality upholding the bourgeois society and legitimizing the various European empires, be they British, German, Austrian, or French.[6]

The work of the Rhenish mission was made particularly difficult—and frequently compromised—by its uncritical acceptance of the colonialist policies of the empire. From the beginning, the mission welcomed the German immigrants. The efforts of Luederitz, the pioneer colonizer who had sought to extend the German empire to include South West Africa, were seen as providential. The mission believed that the tribal wars that dominated early nineteenth-century history would be terminated only by the establishment of a strong European presence in the land.

Friedrich Fabri, director of the Rhenish Mission Society at Barmen, encouraged the settlement of South West Africa by Germans. German emigration would lead to the establishment of an imperial presence in Africa that would both strengthen the prestige of German culture and also bring its advantages to what it regarded as a backward land whose inhabitants seemed hopelessly caught up in intertribal strife. While there were warnings within the mission of the dangers implicit in its being co-opted by colonial interests, it was unthinkable that the mission would advocate political self-determination for the African population. The Rhenish mission attempted instead to define formal political policy along traditional lines respecting a basic distinction between church and state.

> If we now greet the German colony in South Africa with joyful hearts, it is important that we not close our eyes to the misgivings and dangers which are posed for us by the same. First of all, it is important that we ourselves clarify this matter and not allow the obvious recognition that

mission and colonization are two different matters to be obscured by patriotic enthusiasms. Colonization serves to expand the power and reputation of our beloved German fatherland, whereas mission work wishes to serve the expansion of the kingdom and the honor of our heavenly king, Jesus Christ. Hence we do not wish to mix hopelessly together here things that are actually dissimilar nor to confuse them with one another. It will be better for both if they are clearly and distinctly held apart, for history teaches us that nothing good ever comes from missionaries founding colonies or from the colonial power performing mission work.[7]

Nonetheless, a major and potentially ominous qualification was added.

But just as church and state back home are often forced to assist one another and to work hand in hand for the benefit of the entire people, the one showing the required consideration for the other, so it is with the mission and colonization abroad.[8]

The obvious possibility of fundamental conflict between the two institutions was simply not considered.

That is why we must desire from the entire heart, and that is the task for which we and our foreign missionaries as well have warmed our entire hearts, that a peaceful and friendly relationship may exist between mission and colonization. Thus, everywhere it is possible to do so, the one should gladly and willingly support and work hand in hand with the other, so that each shows the proper consideration for the other at all times. That this latter development may actually materialize from the German Empire as a colonial power and for the colonial societies as well is the goal to which our every hope and desire is directed.[9]

The assumption that the two German institutions, church and state, could have no serious difficulty in working "hand in hand" would prove tragically naive. The mission's attempt to distinguish between evangelical and imperial interests was rooted in its understanding of Luther's distinction between God's two kingdoms, the spiritual and the political. But that the mission immediately found itself compelled to abandon its own reformation roots by assuming a natural connection between evangelical and imperial concerns indicates how tenuous its understanding of its heritage actually was. The theoretical interest in recognizing a basic difference between God's political and spiritual "kingdoms," between public order and personal wholeness, would prove merely hypothetical. The former would be removed from evangelical judgment and thus become morally autonomous. The latter would claim to be acultural while demanding, in fact, a substitution of European for African norms for the Christian life.

The belief in the mission's mandate to educate as well as to evangelize the African rested on the unexamined (and theologically dubious) assumption that gospel and culture are inseparable. Furthermore, even for the Africans, the particular culture to be expressed by the spiritual kingdom must be European rather than indigenous. One north German missionary's argument may be regarded as representative.

> The inhabitants of our colonies cannot remain in their natural condition. They are by nature mostly untamed and warlike, whereas the colonial administration wants people in its territory who are orderly, well-bred, and peaceful. The natives are by nature lazy and work no harder than they must, whereas the German planter wants willing and hard-working laborers. The natives are by nature unpretentious, whereas the trader hopes that they will buy all of the beautiful wares which he lays out in his shop—and as payment for these wares, he wants them to bring him as many products of the soil as possible. If the native population is ever to satisfy these desires, they must be raised out of the childlike state in which they presently find themselves to a higher level. They must lay aside their bad manners, just as they must learn how to extract greater yields from the rich tropical soil in order to pay for the "necessities of life" which they have so recently discovered and in order to develop a resistance against the dangers which the European culture is so rapidly bringing down upon them.
>
> In short, the natives must be educated. Here is where the mission steps forward and announces: "That is my task. I am prepared to act as educator in our colonies, just as I have done in other of our Lord's lands." That is not the mission's ultimate and highest purpose. . . . [But] the education of the native inhabitants is, so to speak, a by-product of their Christianization, and it is quite acceptable to the mission that she is able in this way to be of service to the politicians, business interests, and other colonists.[10]

Yet, fleetingly, a caveat was sounded:

> For the sake of her higher purpose, the mission should not undertake common activity together with her fellow-countrymen in secular professions. She must rather—even in individual instances—offer herself as the spokesman for the natives, since she is by her very nature in a better position to gain their confidence.[11]

But the final loyalty in the context would be European. "So much the better, then, that the mission has something to lay on the scales in order to do a great service for her fellow-countrymen."[12]

Significantly, it was easier to see the danger in the tendency to identify European culture and the gospel when displayed by others. Julius Richter declared:

> The antithesis of Kingdom of God and world is becoming a question of conscience for the mission. [Many missions] . . . have been harmed by an unhealthy fusion with international political and business interests, with Anglo-Saxon cultural expansion, and with American secular ideas. We would preserve for the life of the German mission the precious jewel of her pure religious motivation.[13]

In practice the distinction between spiritual and political concerns remained purely formal. As Friedrich Fabri, head of the Rhenish mission, understood it, God's will for society is purely abstract: no content has been disclosed in the sole locus of his revelatory Word, the Bible. One moves in neo-Lutheran pietism from a posture of a theoretical separation of spiritual and political concerns to a self-contradictory policy which, while claiming not to be an ally of any government, yet demands uncritical obedience to whatever policy any specific government proposes even if its legislation violates the most fundamental of human rights. Thus, he argues:

> The church is in no single time or place under any kind of obligation to ally itself too closely with any one particular form of government, especially since governments in this earthly life are of necessity constantly undergoing change. On the contrary, the only obligation which it owes to any political authority that has ever existed and which it owes to any political authority that has been established at any single time is the active offer of obedience, the loyalty which is required of a subject, and in keeping with Paul's important advice in his letter to Timothy—the obligation to make intercession conscientiously for it. Should the Christian's political obligation extend further, and should he himself or the church as a whole be permitted in a Christian sense to meddle in political questions or to choose sides in them, then I really do not know how it would be possible for one to avoid the reproach of God's Word that he has left us entirely without advice in this all important aspect of life. Indeed, if that were allowed according to the Scriptures, then the Scriptures themselves would of necessity have to indicate not only the most ideal form of state but also which state is in itself morally good and which morally bad. But there is so very little evidence of such concern; the Holy Scriptures themselves never directly attack the institution of slavery—an institution which plays such a vital role in the entire socio-

political life today—no matter how diametrically opposed the existence of slavery may be to the sense and spirit of the Scriptures. Thus, even when a political conflict arises over the questions of slavery, a Christian can never substantiate his occasional solidarity with the anti-slavery party on the basis of God's Word.[14]

Thus, biblical literalism inspired by modern nationalistic fervor proposes an interpretation of Reformation ethics that subverts Reformation theology. Instead of preserving the distinction between politics and salvation, the saved are compelled to offer uncritical obedience to the civil authorities. The closest possible identification of the spiritual and the political results—with the word of God so interpreted that it is exluded from influencing the social agenda. The content of Christian political ethics becomes the giving of blanket approval to whatever political administration—however deficient morally—happens to be in power.

It is understandable that the mission would find it difficult to recognize a possible incompatibility between evangelization and colonization even though the mission's two constituencies, the Africans and the Germans, did not understand themselves to share common interests. The Namibian Johannes L. de Vries gives a particularly vivid example of the conflict between the two groups.

[A] major result of colonialism [was] . . . racial discrimination. This was caused by the haughty attitude of the colonial peoples, who despised everything that was not European. Thus, the "negro" is referred to in a derogatory way; he may be used as a laborer but never regarded as an equal. The evil heritage which our generation received from this can be clearly seen in the tensions which still reign in South Africa and Namibia. Here we are still fighting against an unsolved problem of inherited colonialism.[15]

Within the mission itself contradictions between classic doctrine and actual practice proved insurmountable. The Western tradition of political theology was reduced to a legalistic, noncontextual reading of Romans 13:1f. "Let every person be subject to the governing authorities. For there is no authority except from God, and those that exist have been instituted by God." Whenever missionaries in the field would press the political rights of their Namibian flock, the authorities of the mission in Barmen would remind them of the *de facto* political supremacy of the German government. The missionaries were German citizens and owed the Kaiser their obedience. Was it not obvious that to do otherwise would be to violate Romans 13? In South West Africa the situation was seen differently. African Christians had no argument with St. Paul. The problem, rather, was one of interpretation. *Which* authority has God placed over the Namibian people? Their own chiefs or the emperor of Germany? A political theology based exclusively on a noncontextual reading of Romans 13 would dodge the real issue: the contest between tribal and colonial authority. Rarely was the contradiction acknowledged. Agents of the Rhenish mission in Germany repeatedly found it necessary to warn the missionaries on the field that it was their duty to be obedient to the German government and that they should in no way become involved in "political issues" as far as the colonial government was concerned. Advocacy for the tribe was ruled out in principle. The need to issue such warnings suggests that the missionaries were not restricting themselves to purely "spiritual concerns" and that in fact, as pastors of African congregations, they could not in conscience countenance colonial subversion of the welfare of their people.

Historically, the relation of pietism to community life, specifically to political responsibility, has been an ambiguous one. Mary Fulbrook has shown that within German Lutheranism, pietism took dramatically different courses.[16] In both Wuertemberg and Prussia pietistic movements sought "to complete the Reformation" by seeking to transform society through the moral arm of the church so that God's "holy commonwealth on earth" might be established. In the case of seventeenth-century Wuertemberg, pietism actively opposed the absolutist politics of the time by emphasizing the need for Christians to live out a biblically based life of personal moral rigor. The church was sufficiently influenced by the pietist movement that its leadership found it possible to oppose openly the policies of an absolutist government. In eighteenth-century Prussia, however, the government embodied in the provincial nobility was able to co-opt the pietist movement. Lutheran orthodoxy in the church in company with the feudal aristocracy was able to employ the pietist interest in religious and social righteousness in its own program of defending the old social order. Pietism in Prussia came to support absolutism because it seemed to its leaders that this was the only feasible route to achieving their goals.[17] The pietists' emphasis on "practical Christianity" and its relative indifference to sustained, critical reflection on the meaning of theological affirmations does not necessarily make it politically irrelevant. Politically ambiguous pietism, capable of opposing absolutism in Wuertemberg while supporting it in Prussia, would prove politically significant in Africa as well. Pietism transplanted to a quite different environment would flourish, not without being compelled, however, to reexamine its inherited political assumptions.

Very early in the evangelization of Namibia the impossibility, in practice, of separating religion and politics had become obvious. On occasion, the Rhenish mission itself had, in fact, become the center for the economic and political administration of the territory. During the Herero-Nama War of Liberation (1863–70), the old mission at Otjimbingwe had become a center of refuge for both Herero and Europeans. Hugo Hahn had earlier hoped that the development of a mission-sponsored trading center at Otjimbingwe would promote the independence of the African congregations by preventing their exploitation by itinerant traders as well as provide support for the mission's financial needs. However ingenuous the innovation, the mission soon found itself facing unanticipated consequences.

As congregations looked to the mission for economic and political support, the missionaries themselves were increasingly pressed to function as "headmen" of the new Christianized tribes. For many Herero this arrangement seemed natural. "Teacher" (omuhonga) and "headman" (omuhona) were not so very different. In wartime the mission was able to offer protection that the traditional chiefs had become less able to provide. Yet the discomfiture of at least some at the mission is clearly evident in the entry of missionary Schoenberg in his diary for 12 September 1853.

> I do not like to make any new laws. I told [an African] of Genesis 9:6 (Whoever sheds the blood of a man, by man shall his blood be shed). I could not quote Romans 13:4 . . . for there is no effective government here. I said, "Now listen, Kazandu, I am not here for the purpose of punishing human beings. Those murderers, however, must never again be allowed to live in this place. They must know that they cannot behave that way here." He agreed and thus it was to be.[18]

While it would prove difficult to reconcile German and African understandings of justice, their very difference would serve to relativize the German claim to be normative. Disputes concerning the meaning of law implied not that the Africans had no respect for law, but that their legal tradition had a different basis and operated with different assumptions.

Subsequently, when the colonial government became able to assume political authority, the mission was willing to be relieved of that burden. A fracture, however, had appeared in the facade of the mission's position. A religious community that had a theoretical bias against dealing with economic and political issues would find that in an emergency situation it would be required to assume responsibility for more than the purely spiritual nurture of its people. So it was before the establishment of the German colonial authority; so it had been during the years of intertribal strife. So it would be again when it would become' evident that yet another colonial authority had lost its moral credibility.

In spite of its official indifference to politics, the mission, as an institution, was to prove a highly effective political agent. In 1884, the Rhenish mission had been successful in pressing the German government to declare the territory a German Protectorate, believing that "without the presence of the German troops the extension of the Gospel would be impossible."[19] In the perennial conflict between the Nama and the Herero, the mission had sided first with the former, later supporting the latter. It is not necessary to reconstruct the complex detail in forming the mission's shifting strategies of involvements. Though policies might fluctuate, from its beginning the mission was heavily engaged in both intertribal and colonial politics. Whatever its theological claim, the mission was never in practice apolitical. Until the formation of an indigenous church, the political policy of the Rhenish mission was to strengthen the role of the white colonial presence, primarily the German, subsequently the South African, and to weaken the fabric of tribal society.

When the mission determined to establish its own trading company, it inevitably would come to exercise a profound effect on the traditional economy of the nomadic tribes. With the introduction of a money economy along with European goods into African society, the traditional culture would be forever transformed. It was the mission that laid the foundations for the introduction of the Africans into capitalism: the movement of the Africans from traditional religion to Christianity was paralleled by their gradual incorporation into a market economy. The combination of these two conversions would set the Africans on a path of no return. The so-called "modernization of the African peoples" would prove relentless since it provided both material and spiritual challenge to the old traditions. The encouragement given by the mission to the development of a money economy had no basis, of course, in its privatistic, other-worldly theology. Its action, however, was eloquent enough and would prove effective. The mission consistently supported the colonial development of the territory largely because it was inconceivable that its understanding of Christianity could be expressed apart from European economic and political forms. A mission that was formally committed to the spreading of a "pure Gospel" discovered, in practice, that that task could not be pursued without strong support from colonialism's social assumptions.

Christian ethics, in the mission's perspective, did not deal with the moral issues raised by the introduction of European political praxis into African culture. Its policy of silence served, however, to function as the voice of assent. Pietism's unwillingness to deal with social issues at a theological level exposed one of its major weaknesses. Western Christianity has in fact a strong tradition of social theory, classically defined in the medieval and reformation sources that in other respects formed the substance of the pietistic faith. The Rhenish mission's abandoning of the Christian tradition of social ethics created a vacuum into which a simplistic policy of support for German political and commercial interests could enter unchallenged.

The subsequent development in the twentieth century of a cheap, highly controlled labor force as a major component in the country's economy can also be traced back to the beginnings of white settlement. The newly baptized typically left the traditional community and settled in colonies near the mission stations where the missionary became the *de facto* chief. Conversion to Christianity meant in fact a sundering of traditional ties and the entrance into a new "Christian tribe," one that would be sympathetic to the designs of European commercial and political interests. The inability of the mission to discern the conflict of interests involved in its attempt to identify with both German and African communities was ultimately a theological problem. The Reformation doctrine of a divine twofold righteousness, God's reign in justification and justice, had been abandoned at the expense of the latter and the distortion of the former. Ethics, for Rhenish pietism in Namibia, had been reduced to the imposition of a stern morality on the converted, an outward sign demonstrating their separation from the traditions of their ancestors. Only obedience to the emperor, placed over Namibia by God, needed to be added.[20]

The subsequent slaughter of the Herero and Nama people by the imperial forces was, it might have been supposed, an irrefutable demonstration of the inherent incompatibility of colonialist and indigenous interests. But for the mission, even an attempt at genocide could occasion no reassessment of the essential correctness of its loyalty to the empire. It is with disbelief mixed with horror that one reads the pastoral letter of the mission to the pitiful handful of surviving Herero Christians.

Dearly beloved in Christ Jesus,

It is not easy for us to attach such a title to this letter. Our love for you has suffered a rude shock on account of the terrible rebellion in which so many of you took part and on account of the awful bloodshed, as well as the many atrocities associated with the rebellion, for which you also share at least co-responsibility, even if we still hope that only a few of you were directly involved in these atrocious and murderous deeds. But our Saviour's love never ceases. It pursues the lost sinners to save them and make them holy. The father continues to love even the prodigal son who has left his father's house and has trampled upon his father's will, just as he is prepared to forgive the same son as soon as the son returns penitently to the father and says: "Father, I have sinned against heaven and before you and am henceforth no longer worthy to be called your son." It is in this spirit that we continue to refer to you as "dearly beloved in Christ Jesus."

We dare not conceal from you that you have made us very unhappy and have caused us great sorrow. Our heart bleeds when we think of you, as the heart of the father bled when the prodigal son turned his back on him. You too have set out upon a path which will inevitably lead you to misfortune, and you will perish miserably unless you soon recognize your error and repent. You have raised the sword against the government which God has placed over you without considering that it is written, "Whoever takes the sword shall also perish by the sword."[21]

The total identification of the Gospel with the interests of the political establishment made possible a castigation of the defeated—as sentimental as it was cruel. It is indeed on the victims that blame must fall.

While pietism is politically ambiguous, it can commit its followers to significant social activity. For the pietist the world is fully open to moral criticism, and the Christian is expected to address the ills discerned. There are pietistic quietists, of course, but a pietistic activism is also possible. The foreign mission movement itself, with deep roots in pietist soil, is activist in the extreme. Incursion into a foreign culture with the deliberate intent to subvert its values and traditions is hardly a posture of social passivity. It is, in the deepest sense of the word, revolutionary.[22]

In the north, the work of the Finnish Mission Society among the Ovambo people, though also inspired by Lutheran pietism, employed a markedly different approach. The north had not been conquered by the Germans, nor was it part of the German Protectorate. Finland was not a colonial power, nor were its missionaries compromised by attempting to represent the interests of both church and empire. The lack of a German presence in the north gave the Finnish mission the freedom necessary to pursue its ends apart from imperial pressure. Particularly significant was its demonstration of the competence of the mission to work effectively without the protection of a white military force—inconceivable to the Rhenish society. While the Finnish mission inevitably represented the culture of northeastern Europe, its devotion to the well-being of the Ovambo people was so uncompromised that its work was not perceived as a threat to Ovambo identity. The resentment aroused by the German mission's double loyalty to Gospel and empire was avoided in the north. The fruitfulness of its work is well attested in the formation of what has come to be the largest church in the country. Again, the ambiguity of pietism's theology is evident. On one hand, traditional themes were sounded: the message of the church is nothing other than the content of the Bible as interpreted by nineteenth-century European pietism. The burden of proclamation is an explication of Scripture that exhorts the congregation to enter the way of salvation and to live an exemplary Christian life. That legacy proved both effective and durable. An analysis of Namibian sermons shows that preaching typically focused on the classic themes of the creation and the fall, the nature of sin, and the promise of salvation through Christ's atonement, the profile of the Christian life as a fight against sin and evil, and the transcendent hope of eternal life.[23] Daily life is characteristically seen as a struggle. Kalunga has been reinterpreted as the ever-present Christ, the shepherd of his new tribe, the Christian community. A general insensitivity to the collective character of the life of faith as set forth in the Old and New Testaments, in spite of their strong affinity for the African sense of social solidarity, is striking, but, as we shall see, did not prove irreparable. The biblical emphasis on the community as the context for personal faith was rarely made explicit, although for the hearers, if not for the preachers, that may be assumed as obvious. As in the south, the powers that be are indeed ordained by God. In the north those powers did not refer to representatives of the German empire, however. As a result, the dignity and authority of the tribal leaders were not undercut by the mission. In a future generation, when it might become necessary to question the legitimacy and justice of another colonial power, the Ovambo would not see themselves as impious rebels, but as an oppressed people with a legitimate and divine claim for the rectification of gross injustice. Thus, while pietism can preach both a message of patience in the face of suffering and an apolitical indifference bordering on irresponsibility it can also, as among the Ovambo, serve to champion the oppressed, recognizing the legitimacy of a community's natural leadership as a creation of God. It is not entirely accidental, perhaps, that the nation's primary liberation movement,

SWAPO (South West Africa People's Organization), would spring from Ovambo soil.[24]

After World War II, the two large black churches with a reformation heritage were the first in the country to become autonomous. In 1954 the Finnish mission became the Evangelical Lutheran Ovambokavango Church (ELOC). The Right Reverend Leonard Auala became its first Namibian moderator in 1960 and was consecrated bishop in apostolic succession in 1963. The Rhenish mission established the Evangelical Lutheran Church South West Africa (ELCSWA) in 1957, with Pastor Paulus Gowaseb as its first African moderator. That the largest African churches were able to begin work under an indigenous leadership already in the 1950s was to prove critical. Their new administrative structures contradicted apartheid on two counts. The formation of the ELCSWA was particularly distressing to the South African government, since the church's membership was inclusive of a variety of ethnic groups. According to apartheid, each group is to be separate: pan-African organizations violate the grand design. Without specifically opposing South African rule, the mere existence of a large, racially inclusive community was an affront to government policy.

A second, more subtle, but no less significant, factor also emerged: blacks now demonstrated the capacity to administer large, complex organizations that articulate a philosophy and program that implicitly contradict government policy. That blacks may be Christian had not been denied by the government. But that blacks can be "masters in their own house," that they can build and administer their own polities without supervision by whites was a *de facto* demonstration of the political irrationality of government policy. Even where there was no public protest against apartheid, the very existence of strong black churches—albeit the result of the work of supposedly apolitical missionaries—constituted a direct threat to the policies of "the powers that be." African political movements have made it possible for the people to obtain opportunity for political action both in Namibia itself and in the international community. Not only did the rank and file of these movements come from the churches; many of its founders and its leadership have been teachers in the churches' schools.

A New Colonialism

In August 1914, three days after the outbreak of World War I, Great Britain ordered the Union of South Africa to take steps to seize the German colony to its northwest, German South West

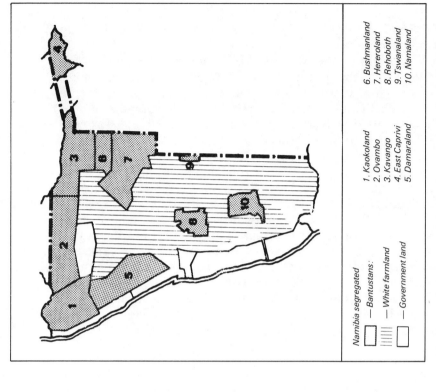

LAND USAGE IN NAMIBIA

Rundu

Onopoho

Tsumeb

Oljiwarongo

Gobabis

Windhoek

Kalahari

Mariental

Keetmans-
hoop

Namib

Swakopmund
Walvis Bay

Lüderitz

— *Desert*

— *Semi-desert, scarce vegetation with goats and sheep breeding*

— *Dry savanna (grass and thorn shrubs) with cattle breeding*

— *Dry savanna (grass and trees) with cultivation and smallstock*

— *Cultivation and intensive stock breeding with irrigation*

Namibia segregated

— *Bantustans:*

— *White farmland*

— *Government land*

1. Kaokoland	*6. Bushmanland*
2. Ovambo	*7. Hereroland*
3. Kavango	*8. Rehoboth*
4. East Caprivi	*9. Tswanaland*
5. Damaraland	*10. Namaland*

Apartheid Restricts the African Population. (*Courtesy of IDAF.*)

Africa.[25] By July 1915, Union troops were able to compel the
Germans to capitulate, bringing the colony under an interim military government. During the balance of World War I, the presence
of British-controlled South African troops in the colony inevitably
evoked hope that with the victory of the allies, freedom might come
to the land. That was not to happen, but the possibilities of liberty,
suddenly renewed, would not be quickly forgotten. With the signing
of the peace treaty at Versailles in June of 1919, the political
complexity of the colony's future began to become apparent. The
British and their surrogates, the representatives of the Union of
South Africa, vigorously pressed for the annexation of South West
Africa, arguing that the former German possession should be incorporated as a fifth province in the Union of South Africa.

The Americans, under Woodrow Wilson, adamantly opposed the
British proposal. The contest was finally resolved by declaring the
territory a South African mandate. Article twenty-two of the new
League of Nations Covenant had made provision for the administration of former colonies whose inhabitants were judged not yet
ready to assume the responsibilities of self-government. Various
member states of the League of Nations entered into mandate
agreements with the league to administer the former colonies in
preparation for their political independence "as a sacred trust of
civilization." In the case of South West Africa, a "class C" mandate was designed to permit the former German colony to be
administered as an integral portion of the Union of South Africa,
subject to the interests of the inhabitants and to the consent of the
other league members. The Wilsonian concern for the right of self-
determination thrust the United States into a theater of responsibility where it previously had had no involvement. Wilson's argument would prove fateful. The American commitment to national
self-determination would collide with the presumed competence of
imperial administrators to know how to serve the best interests of
the indigenous population. The credibility of Wilson's principle,
however, would be established only when the international community would acknowledge its responsibility for the implementation of this particular "sacred trust."

While the league had established a monitoring mechanism, the
Union of South Africa, for all practical purposes, was largely free to
superimpose its own political philosophy and economic policy on
the mandated territory. Under a "C" mandate, the Union authorities were given administrative and legislative powers of the
territory permitting the governance of the former German colony as
though it were an integral part of the Union itself. True, certain

requirements had to be met: slavery was prohibited; freedom of religion was guaranteed. Restrictions concerning forced labor, military training, and munitions traffic were levied. The Union government was required to submit an annual report to the Council of the League. And above all, the Union was charged to "promote to the utmost the material and moral well being and the social progress of the inhabitants."[26] Under the mandate, South Africa's obligation to report to the League of Nations had no provision for comment by the Africans themselves. In actual practice, the mandate was regarded as a formality by the British and the South Africans; the incorporation of the territory into the Union proceeded apace. Between 1920 and 1923, South Africa was able to subdue the northern part of the country, including the major portion of Ovamboland, an area beyond the old German protectorate. Thus, Ovamboland itself was permanently divided between Portugal and South Africa; the Ovambo, the region's largest group, would become wards of two different colonial powers.

With the end of the German occupation, the Herero had requested the return of their lands. They were given instead a portion of the sand veld where thousands of Herero had perished in 1904. Far from the British victory bringing a new dispensation, the South African administration established new laws to restrict the political rights of the Africans still further. In 1922 legislation was passed to assure a cheap labor supply: Africans leaving assigned work areas would be punished for vagrancy; all blacks traveling outside assigned "home areas" were required to carry documentation showing police approval. When this legislation was challenged by the league, it was discovered that there was no mechanism by which the Union—or implicitly the empire—could be prevented from putting it into force. Rebellion and rumors of rebellion were common. In 1922 over a hundred Nama were killed by South African troops using machine guns and military aircraft because they had refused to pay a new tax levied on their hunting dogs![27]

However intense the hostility between the English and the German-speaking elements in the white community during the war, at the armistice it was possible quickly to close ranks lest the African leaders effectively press claims for self-determination or the restoration of lands. Old tribal land was in part sold to new settlers from South Africa and in part returned to resident Germans. The major administrative change assigned the old British port, Walvis Bay, to the Union of South Africa, thus signaling the intent to integrate further South West Africa into South Africa proper.

During the years between the world wars, South African policy increasingly sought to administer the territory as an integral part of the Union. In 1922 a Native Administration Proclamation ordered all Africans living in the areas of white settlement (the so-called police zone of the German period) to be confined to reserves and to be subject to pass requirements. In 1925 a contract labor system was introduced by which the central government was able to establish, as formal policy, what had been common practice for decades: workers from the north, who made up half of the country's surviving black population, could be recruited to leave their families to become laborers in the mines and on farms in the south. In the same year white settlers were given political representation in a legislative assembly sitting in Windhoek; the Africans, of course, were excluded.

The United Nations contra South Africa

With the formation of the United Nations in May 1945 the old Permanent Mandates Commission of the League of Nations was replaced by a less accommodating Trusteeship Commission that would prove to be considerably more responsive to the political aspirations of the newly emerging African states. The Union of South Africa, on the other hand, served notice that since from its perspective, the League of Nations' mandate had lapsed, the United Nations could not be regarded as the legal successor of the league, and that, in any case, the Union was now prepared to take final steps to make South West Africa its fifth province. Strong support for this strategy was given by South West African whites, including the Germans, even though they had been disenfranchised by the Union during the war. Somewhat as an afterthought, the Union government subsequently sponsored a series of public meetings in late 1945 and early 1946 for the African population, seeking to obtain their support for incorporation as well. On the basis of its findings, the government concluded, quite unremarkably, that the Africans too desired incorporation into the Union.

In 1946 South Africa, under the leadership of Jan Christian Smuts, again applied to the United Nations for formal permission to incorporate South West Africa into the Union. Chiefs Hosea Kutako, Frederick Maharero, and Samuel Hendrik Witbooi protested in the name of their people. The Anglican missionary, the Reverend Michael Scott, was delegated by Kutako to plead the Africans' cause at the United Nations. While the South African government objected to what it took to be unwarranted interference

South African Police Break up a SWAPO Demonstration. *(Courtesy of IDAF.)*

A Mass Grave for the Victims of the Cassinga Massacre. *(Courtesy of IDAF.)*

by the church in what was for them a strictly political matter, Father Scott was able to alert the international community to its responsibility to give far greater attention to the views of the indigeneous population than it had in the past.

Meanwhile, a dramatic political transformation, a nonviolent revolution, had swept over the Union. In 1948 the Afrikaner-dominated National party came to power in South Africa under the leadership of the Calvinist theologian, the Reverend Dr. D. F. Malan. The Union began to prepare itself to become a republic, politically independent of Britain. Ten white members from South West Africa were seated in the Union House of Assembly and Senate and South West Africa was declared to be no longer subject to the provisions of the League of Nations' mandate. South Africa was now prepared to proceed on its own initiative to incorporate the old German colony into its own political structure. Accordingly, South Africa informed the Trustee Council of the United Nations that it would no longer submit annual reports on its administration of South West Africa. The International Court of Justice declared in July 1950, however, that annual reports would indeed be required from South Africa and that it could not alter the status of a trust territory without U.N. approval. The issue thus was joined: the international community holding South Africa accountable for its administration of the former mandate by preparing it for independence versus South Africa declaring that it was sovereign in determining the political destiny of South West Africa.

It seemed clear that South Africa would prevail. After World War II the economic development of Namibia under South African and international corporations had increased dramatically. The territory had become totally subordinated to South African economic interests. In order to supervise a more vigorous application of apartheid, a South West Native Affairs Administration Act was enacted in 1954, requiring that the African population in the territory be regulated henceforth by administrative officers in Pretoria rather than in Namibia itself. Thus in 1959, demonstrating its intent to extend its apartheid policy in its "fifth province," the South African government announced the destruction of the traditional housing area for Africans in Windhoek. They would be compelled to move to a bleak, military-style township, Katatura, several miles north of the city. At a protest meeting called by the African leaders of the township, it was pointed out that housing costs would be nearly twelve times greater in Katatura and all housing would now be owned by the government. The speakers were eloquent in their opposition. Then suddenly, without warning the police appeared armed with sten guns. When the crowd refused to disperse, the police opened fire, killing eleven and wounding forty-four, two of whom subsequently died.[28]

Within the black community, opposition to South Africa's strategy would prove vigorous and unrelenting. An Ovamboland People's Organization (OPA) had been organized in 1957 among contract workers, largely Ovambo, to compel reform of the servile conditions under which they were forced to work.[29] The South West African National Union (SWANU) was established in May 1959 under Herero leadership as another liberationist party, but has been unable to develop a national constituency. In 1960, OPO changed its name to the South West Africa People's Organization (SWAPO), in part to recognize the importance of its increasingly national rather than Ovambo membership, and in part to reflect the importance of emphasizing its ultimate objection, the creation of a politically united nation. The following year SWAPO established its military wing, the People's Liberation Army of Namibia (PLAN), in the belief that political action by itself would not be sufficient to compel South Africa to leave the country.

South Africa's ultimate design for Namibia's future was disclosed in December of 1963 when the Odendaal Commission, named after its chair, F. H. Odendaal of the Transvaal, published its five-year plan for the complete implementation of apartheid in Namibia. Nine homelands (reservations) were to be established for the blacks: Ovamboland, Okavangoland, Kaokoveld, East Caprivi, Damaraland, Namaland, Hereroland, Bushmanland, and Tswanaland, plus one for one colored community, Rehoboth. The three white communities and other coloreds would be permitted to live in the rest of the country. Thus, a nation that at that time had less than a million inhabitants would be divided into eleven unequal parts. All viable farming land, the rich mineral deposits (including the diamonds), and the extensive fishing rights were to be reserved for one of the country's smallest minorities, the whites. The homelands were to be located far removed from the towns and industrial sites, thus insuring further provision for white control.

There is no doubt that many in the South African government believed that the establishment of the homelands would convince the world at large that such an arrangement would enable each ethnic group to preserve its own identity and thus be able to achieve some day a measure of self-determination. The actual impact of the policy on the Namibian people as human beings seems, however, not to have been calculated. The population would be divided into eleven separate groups, each assigned separate housing, employment, and marital regulations. All members of the three white groups, each fiercely determined to keep its identity separate from the other two, would be permitted to have access to the large "white" portions of the country. The "colored" community, with the exception of the Rehoboth Basters, would not have a separate homeland, but would be assigned locations usually near "white" towns.

The sense of national unity that had been developing during the German period would now be suppressed: blacks in particular, should be encouraged to develop loyalty to their relatively small tribal groups rather than to the country as a whole. Citizenship in the nation would be out of the question for blacks; that would be the prerogative of the whites. Among major economic consequences of the homeland policy would be its policy of providing a continuing supply of cheap African labor for the white economy since the Africans could not be supported on the small arid homelands to which they had been assigned.

Tribal governments would be supported by the white authorities to maintain control in the homelands. The old policy of divide and rule would be most effective if actual rule were delegated to local tribal chiefs who could be persuaded to discern personal profit in cooperating with the South African government. The specific forms of apartheid had varied over the years, but the basic design was clear: the allocation of educational, medical, and employment opportunities on a discriminatory but legally valid racial basis.

Meanwhile, at the international level, the liberation movement suffered a particularly severe blow. In 1966 the International Court of Justice, after protracted, complex litigation, ruled that Ethiopia and Liberia, the sole African members of the old League of Nations, were not competent to object to South Africa's colonization of Namibia. The Hague court held that the plaintiffs had failed to demonstrate sufficient legal interest in the case to compel a ruling that would censure South Africa. The General Assembly, reflecting the astonished reaction widely expressed in the international community, proposed a new strategy. On 27 October 1966 the General Assembly acted to terminate South Africa's mandatory powers, once and for all. It announced that it

[d]eclares that South Africa has failed to fulfill its obligations in respect of the administration of the Mandated Territory and to ensure the moral and material well-being and security of the indigenous inhabitants of South West Africa and has, in fact, disavowed the Mandate;

Decides that the Mandate conferred upon His Britannic Majesty to be exercised on his behalf by the government of the Union of South Africa is therefore terminated, that South Africa has no other right to administer the Territory, and that henceforth South West Africa comes under the direct responsibility of the United Nations.[30]

South Africa, of course, immediately rejected the United Nations' action: the General Assembly had merely demonstrated its own incompetence in attempting to interfere in the republic's internal affairs.

The following spring the General Assembly demonstrated its seriousness by establishing an eleven-member U.N. Council for South West Africa. The council was authorized to establish appropriate administrative offices in the territory, to arrange for the departure of South African government personnel, to create a legislature based on national elections in which the whole population would be represented, and to assist the new nation to draw up its own constitution. What was most important, the council "shall do all in its power to enable independence to be attained by June 1968."[31] The brave new birth of hope was to be quickly aborted, however, The major Western powers abstained from action authorizing the Security Council to enable the council to carry out its new assignment. A gesture, although important in itself, was to be the sole achievement of June 1968. The council was renamed the Council for Namibia in recognition of the usage already common in liberationist circles. An African nation would no longer be burdened by its colonial designation. The new name, based on an old African word for "shield," would symbolize the struggle that lay ahead.

Though long reluctant to enter the lists, the Security Council slowly began to show more resolve. In the preceding year, thirty-seven Namibians had been transported to South Africa to stand trial under new legislation that had been made retroactive in 1962. The Security Council condemned the trial as illegal and demanded that the prisoners be released and be permitted to return to their own country. South Africa rejected the ruling and immediately brought eight additional Namibians to South Africa to face trial.

Troubled by the continued defiance of U.N. authority, the Security Council appealed to the International Court of Justice to determine the legality of its termination of the old League of Nations' Mandate. On 21 June 1971 the court took historic action declaring that (1) the continued presence of South Africa in Namibia is illegal and it is under obligation to withdraw immediately, (2) members of the United Nations are under obligation to refrain from any dealings with South Africa that might imply recognition of its presence in Namibia, and (3) it is also incumbent on nonmember nations to support this judgment. While the Security Council and the General Assembly welcomed the court's finding, South Africa announced that it rejected the ruling and that it would continue to exercise its control over Namibia.

Within Namibia itself the news of the court's action was electrifying. Although the United Nations had proven unable to deliver independence in 1968, the international community had finally given its legal approval to the Namibian struggle for national freedom. Subsequent negotiations by United Nations' staff in New York, Geneva, Pretoria, and Windhoek to implement the court's action proved fruitless. South Africa remained free to implement its own policies. In principle, Namibia would be required to parallel South Africa in design: Africans would be restricted to their *bantustans* from where they would be pressed into service for white-owned mines and farms. Apartheid might be modified in detail, but it would continue to mean white control of society and not merely separateness. For that to work, draconian measures would be required, insuring both the segregation of whites from blacks and tribes from tribes. And that would mean that blacks could never have political responsibility for sharing in the governing of their own nation.

The frustration suffered by the United Nations in its dealings with South Africa came to a head in December 1973 when it declared SWAPO to be "the authentic representative of the Namibian people." South Africa was outraged. SWAPO, as the most inclusive party in the country, was also South Africa's most formidable opponent.

United Nations censure of South Africa and its recognition of SWAPO would soon prove to have limited immediate effect. The three major Western powers, the United Kingdom, France, and the United States, would repeatedly use their power of veto to protect South Africa from any punitive action imposed by the Security Council. It seemed increasingly clear to the Namibian people that whatever the position of the General Assembly, the major Western powers would not abandon their significant investment in the economy of South Africa and Namibia. For economic and strategic reasons, the West's leading powers would prove to be more interested in preserving the political status quo than in encouraging a fundamental transformation of Namibian society. Nonetheless, SWAPO would receive limited financial aid from a variety of European states, both East and West, and from international church agencies.[32] The major Western powers, while recognizing the need for change in Southern Africa, believed that since South Africa was the dominant political force in the region, it would need to be the chief architect of any new dispensation. And South Africa, terrified by the specter of being surrounded by black, Marxist-oriented states, was determined that Namibia be preserved as a buffer on the west.

Perhaps the old dream of the territory becoming a fifth province would have to be abandoned after all. But could not a technically independent Namibia continue to be dominated politically by South Africa? The republic could insist on the creation of new political structures that would leave the force of South Africa's power undeflected. The only major obstacle to such a design was the Namibian people themselves—particularly if they chose to identify themselves with ethnically inclusive SWAPO. From the South African perspective, it would be inadmissible for SWAPO to participate in the formation of a new Namibia, since SWAPO could not be controlled by South Africa. Unlike the tribal chiefs and a variety of South African-funded splinter groups, SWAPO would not be Pretoria's puppet.

To eliminate SWAPO from the playing field, a triple strategy was developed. While so-called internal SWAPO, as a legitimate political party within the country, could not be made to disappear, it could be weakened. South African spokesmen have repeatedly acknowledged that if national elections were permitted, SWAPO would register a landslide victory. Thus, it would be important that nationwide elections based on the old "one man-one vote" formula not be permitted. Black votes cannot be used to govern white interests.

Secondly, it would be critical to turn world opinion against SWAPO and so blunt the support it receives in the international community. The obvious way to do that was to charge that SWAPO is a communist front. If a postcolonial Namibia can be portrayed as a base for Soviet domination of Southern Africa, support for SWAPO in the West would quickly diminish. Thirdly, as the most powerful military force on the continent, South Africa would need to engage in aggressive warfare against its SWAPO opponents, both those resident in Namibia, as well as expatriates who have fled to neighboring African states. Each of these strategies has had its difficulties. But taken together they have proven, for the time being, to be successful. The only changes permitted are those that Pretoria initiates or agrees to. South Africa does not reject the possibility of an "internationally acceptable settlement"; it is determined, however, that there be no scenario that would allow the massive popular support given SWAPO by the Namibian people to be permitted to place SWAPO in power after independence.

South Africa's identification of SWAPO with communism is of major concern to the West. Rhetoric designed for local consumption portrays South Africa as the continent's primary defender of Christian democratic values—in spite of the sustained criticism of the government's white supremacy policy by the major Catholic and Protestant communities. More effective is the argument that since South Africa is vigorously anti-Communist, any threat to its political domination could give Marxism an opening. Thus, SWAPO's credibility is at stake. There is no doubt that the tendency in both Moscow and Washington to reduce every international conflict to a struggle between the two superpowers seriously damages SWAPO's capacity to gain the sustained international support it needs. The democratic socialist countries of Western Europe have been far more willing to back SWAPO than has the United States. As for SWAPO's supposed communist leanings, assessments by the nation's leading churchmen merit serious attention. Bishop Kleopas Dumeni of Oniipa in northern Namibia could not be more forthright.

I know that the South African government makes propaganda that they are fighting communism. It is propaganda. Who is SWAPO? Let me tell you. SWAPO are members, men and women, daughters and sons of our families, members of our churches. I said churches, regardless of denomination. Baptized, confirmed, married with rights in their parishes. They are Christians. But the question is why they left the country. Precisely the same because of the hardships of the war situation, apartheid, separate development and injustice. And that is what is not Christian. It is against the whole of Christianity.[33]

The former head of the Council of Churches in Namibia, Lutheran Pastor Albertus Maasdorp, is just as pointed.

The South African government has tried to convince the West that their fight in Southern Africa is a holy war against communism. This is not true. Their war is a war against Christ. It is not a war against communism—that is a smokescreen. I sympathize with your concern for Soviet expansion, but the conflict has nothing to do with our struggle for independence. . . . We in the churches of Namibia have no evidence that can make us believe that SWAPO is communist or an agent of communism. We are concerned about our people who are in the movement because the majority in the movement are Lutherans, Catholics,

Anglicans. If SWAPO is labeled as anything, it is to be labeled a national liberation movement.[34]

Clearly, SWAPO is more than a political party. And like other national liberation movements, it has found it necessary to use military force to achieve its goals. But since the great bulk of SWAPO's membership are active members of the church, a moral question arises: May Christians resort to arms for political ends when all else fails? Andimba Toivo Ya Toivo, SWAPO's founder,[35] has offered the representative rationale.

> There are some who will say they are sympathetic with our aims, but that they condemn violence. I would answer that I am not by nature a man of violence, and I believe that violence is a sin against God and my fellowman. SWAPO itself was a non-violent organization. But the South African government is not truly interested in whether opposition is violent or non-violent. It does not wish to hear any opposition to apartheid . . . [To my people] I had no answer to the question, "Where has your non-violence got us?" Whilst the World Court's judgment was pending I at least had that to fall back on. When we failed, after years of waiting, I had an answer to give my people. Even though I did not agree that people should go into the bush [to fight], I could not refuse to help them. . . . Another man might have been able to say, "I will have nothing to do with that sort of thing." I was not, and could not remain a spectator in the struggle of my people for their freedom.[36]

Thus, one of the classic "justifiable war" arguments has proven salient: armed conflict may be a last resort, employed only after all peaceful means have been exhausted. Since none of the churches involved with SWAPO is pacifist, Ya Toivo's argument has proven persuasive for their members.

Meanwhile, the government itself has employed a calculated mix of material blandishments and systematic repression to discourage support for SWAPO among the people. The resources of South Africa's political machinery have been dedicated to the destruction of the organization: bannings, arrests, imprisonment, and exile of its leaders have had their effect. They have also served to toughen the resolve of the liberationists.

The achievement of independence by Angola in 1975 provoked a dramatic escalation in South Africa's investment in the struggle. Namibia, especially the north, became the first line of offense against its newly free, Marxist-inclined neighbor. Within Namibia the long-term strategy of the South African government has continued apace: the creation of an economically dependent, if finally politically independent nation organized along strictly separate racial lines. The so-called Turnhalle principles (named after a Windhoek gymnasium that had been pressed into service as a conference center in the late 1970s) placed major responsibility for the governing process on a second tier ethnic level that would effectively segregate education, health, and police services into separate racial units. A white-dominated first tier would be responsible for national defense and foreign affairs, while a third tier would administer towns and country districts. SWAPO and the churches have consistently opposed the Turnhalle principles as being only a new design for continuing South African politically legitimated racial segregation.

Using Namibia as its staging area, South Africa began, in 1975, to launch a sequence of military intrusions into Angola. The republic has had two major objectives: to supply military support for UNITA (Union for the Total Independence of Angola), its Angolan ally, in seeking the overthrow of the Angolan government, and to destroy SWAPO bases in Angola that could conceivably be used to oppose South African forces. On Ascension Day 1978, South Africa demonstrated the intensity of its anti-SWAPO commitment.

For a number of years thousands of Namibians have chosen to flee their country rather than live under South African rule. Angola, Zambia, and Tanzania have built large refugee centers. At Cassinga, Angola, 156 miles north of the Namibian border, a refugee camp for several thousand Namibian exiles had been established—mostly women, the aged, teenagers, and children. A limited number of armed personnel were stationed at Cassinga for defensive purposes. Early in the morning on 4 May 1978, without warning, the South African Detention Force launched its devastating attack. Jets swept in from Namibia, bombed, strafed, and circled back to drop phosphorous bombs on the camp. Helicopters landed some 200 paratroopers who quickly sprang into action. A wild frenzy of shooting engulfed the camp, stopping only when 612 people lay dead: 298 children, 167 women, and 147 unarmed male civilians.[37] Another 200 were unaccounted for—perhaps fleeing and perishing in the bush. Only 12 SWAPO soldiers defending the camp were killed, giving lie to the subsequent claim by South Africa that Cassinga was a military installation threatening the security of Namibia. Before retreating, the soldiers had the dead hastily dumped into two mass graves.

An additional 611 were wounded. Some 200 survivors, all noncombatants, were rushed to a secret military installation at Mariental in southern Namibia where they were subjected to torture as a part of the army's interrogation procedure.[38] They were released six months later, but only after urgent representations by bishops and relatives of the prisoners had reached the attention of the media. Visiting the remains of the camp later in May, representatives of the U.N. High Commission for Refugees and the World Health Organization reported, "This can only be described as criminal in international law, and barbaric from a moral point of view. It reminds one of the darkest episodes in modern history."[39] In South Africa the Cassinga massacre was celebrated as a victory over "SWAPO terrorists."

The brutality of the attack can be understood as a massive effort to break the morale of SWAPO and, in particular, to make clear that even in exile its members are subject to South African terror. Attacks on Namibians living in Angola and Zambia have become an essential element in South Africa's anti-SWAPO policy. South Africa's inability to govern Namibia in an orderly fashion has driven it to military incursions against its neighbors.

A breakthrough in the settlement of the Namibian issue seemed close in late September 1978. The U.N. Security Council adopted a plan submitted by an interested Contact Group of five Western powers (the United Kingdom, Canada, France, the United States, and West Germany) which again declared the South African occupation of Namibia to be illegal. It went on to call for the creation of a U.N. Transitional Assistance Group "to ensure the early independence of Namibia with free and fair elections under the supervision and control of the United Nations." This plan, U.N. SC Resolution 435 was, in fact, initially accepted by South Africa. However, in December 1978, South Africa chose to conduct its own elections in the territory in violation of Resolution 435.

Since 1978 Namibian political history has been a tortuously protracted exercise in delay and reconsideration. A variety of concessions have been demanded by the republic as prerequisite to the implementation of SCR 435. A joint Contact Group-South Africa conference attempted to resolve remaining difficulties in January 1981, but ended in collapse when South Africa walked out, protesting the "partiality" of the United Nations in favor of SWAPO. Again in 1984 South Africa agreed to an implementation of Resolution 435, but subsequently withdrew from the negotiations.

In July 1988 yet another attempt was made, this time under American aegis. Mounting casualties suffered by white South African troops in Angola, coupled with increasing dissension within the South African government between the traditionally dominant "hawkish" military establishment, and the more "dovish" office of foreign affairs, had served to encourage South Africa to enter the proposed series of talks. While the Soviet Union and the United States, in a new spirit of cooperation, had agreed that there be a Southern African "settlement" in September 1988, the tenth anniversary of Resolution 435's adoption, the Cuban presence in Angola was again linked to the South African occupation of Namibia. The complexity of the negotiations presupposed that the American policy of "constructive engagement" would finally bear fruit: the United States would be able to persuade South Africa to reverse its previous policy. But until South Africa would come to see that its own interests would be best served by the withdrawal of its troops from Namibia, as well as from Angola, little significant change was likely.

In the meantime, South Africa has continued its armed attacks on its African neighbors: Botswana, Lesotho, Mozambique, Zimbabwe, and more especially Angola. The occupation of Namibia thus is seen as a part of a master strategy: South Africa's formidable power, both economic and military, is prepared to defend its traditional domination of Southern Africa. A Namibian settlement is neither necessary nor desirable for the maintenance of that power.

While the United States occasionally affirms its support of Resolution 435, its policy, as demonstrated by its actions, has been in recent years one of support for South Africa's Namibian strategy. A program of "constructive engagement" with South Africa has been designed to strengthen what are perceived as the United States' interests. A mutually supportive alliance with South Africa is seen as necessary for the United States, since South Africa is the primary outpost of anticommunism in Africa, the source of a variety of strategic minerals required by the United States, the dynamic center of the modified free enterprise system dominant in Southern Africa, and the master of the sea-lanes between the South Atlantic and the Indian oceans. Human rights violations are regarded as regrettable, but are not to be permitted to queer the nation's primary foreign policy interests. Although there appears to be an increasing willingness in the Congress and the media to question the nation's South Africa policy, the Republic of South Africa has continued to be, in company with its North American ally, the primary obstacle to the independence of Namibia. Thus, the nation that prevented South Africa from incorporating South West Africa into its political structure in 1919 has become the guarantor of its *de facto* annexation.

3

An African Vision

A Legacy Discovered

> I think South Africa is the most possessing, poignant place I
> have ever seen. I have not been able to get it out of my mind
> since. It is a stereotype destroyer. It is also a profoundly lami-
> nated place that reveals evermore interesting and surprising
> truths about itself as you probe.
>
> —Meg Greenfield

The career of Christianity in Southern Africa has yielded more than
its share of surprises. The *de facto* established church of the most
powerful nation on the continent dominates the moral culture of the
region by means of a rigorous, if probably specious interpretation
of the Calvinist Reformation. The secularization of the West has
not, at least as yet, found a home in Southern Africa, where religion
provides justification of a social system the rest of the world views
with moral abhorrence.

It is also true that a majority of the population of South Africa's
colony, Namibia, finds that a different version of Reformation theology repudiates apartheid's claim to enjoy the support of conservative Protestantism. Perhaps a greater surprise to a secular age
is the discovery that theological arguments, stemming from the
origins of Protestantism, could prove crucial for the political destiny of a major portion of the African continent. Only when religion
has become privatized by either pietist or rationalist sentiment
does Africa's symbiosis of religion and politics seem peculiar. The
African assumption that religion and politics are inseparable aspects of a people's spiritual life is, of course, anticipated everywhere in the biblical literature and was vigorously emphasized in
the recovery of biblical thought commended by the Protestant
Reformers. In Namibia, however, Reformation churches provide the
religious rationale for both the defenders and the opponents of
apartheid. The split between alternative understandings of the Re-

76

formation, however academic it might seem in the modern West, has become central in the struggle for the Namibian future.

Surprises can also be dilemmas. They invite reflection not only for those who seek to understand Namibia, but for those who wonder what significance Namibia may have for the rest of us.

How did the Reformers view the world? Or, more to the point, how did the founders of Southern Africa's major Protestant churches understand the world in which they found themselves? As the South African sociologist T. Dunbar Moodie has shown, the substance of the civil religion that dominates Southern Africa is derived from the Calvinism of its major white population group, the Afrikaners.[1] But this is odd. John Calvin was no racist, nor can support for racism be found in his writings. How then can apartheid spring from Calvinist soil? Moodie points out that belief in the religious basis of national life is central to South African culture.

> The divine agent of the Afrikaner civil faith is Christian and Calvinist— an active sovereign God who calls the elect, who promises and punishes, who brings forth life from death in the course of history. The object of his saving activity—the Afrikaner People—is not a church, a community of the saved, however; it is a whole nation with its distinct language and culture, its own history and special destiny.[2]

What this explicitly religious ideology may lack in theological subtlety is more than compensated for in political relevance. Few have expressed its possibilities more vividly than the Reformed domine, D. F. Malan, who served as prime minister from 1948 to 1954.

> Our history is the greatest masterpiece of the centuries. We hold this nationhood as our due for it was given us by the Architect of the universe. The last hundred years have witnessed a miracle behind which must lie a divine plan. Indeed, the history of the Afrikaner reveals a will and a determination which makes one feel that Afrikanerdom is not the work of men but the creation of God.[3]

In the South African context there is an element in this civil religion that derives from specifically Dutch sources. Developing the neo-Calvinist doctrine of the Dutch theologian, Abraham Kuyper, that God exercises his authority in "individual social spheres" (e.g., family life, science, business, and the arts), the South African theologian, H. G. Stoker, argued that God had created each people with its "separate social sphere," its own structure and purpose. Thus the Afrikaner people were, by God's design, "sovereign in their own circle" and needed to acknowledge no other master than God. Accordingly he reasoned:

> Thus far [God] has preserved the identity of our people. Such preservation was not for naught, for God allows nothing to happen for naught. He might have allowed our people to be bastardized with the native tribes as happened with other Europeans. He did not allow it. He might have allowed us to be anglicized, like for example, the Dutch in America. . . . He did not allow that either. He maintained the identity of our people. He has a future task for us, a calling laid away. . . . If we get our free republic, then it will not be from the hand of man, but will be a gift of God.[4]

In his book, *Credo van 'n Afrikaner,* the South African theologian A. P. Treurnich concluded that since each nation and generation has its own character, apartheid is the natural consequence of the doctrine of creation. The protection of the ethnic "purity" of each nation is God's intent. Thus apartheid, at its roots, is not a secular ideology nor mere political expediency. As Charles Villa-Vicencio, another South African clergyman, has pointed out, apartheid is "grounded in a particular theological outlook of life: a doctrine of creation, a redemptive view of history, a cultural theology, and a natural calling."[5]

Significantly, the Lutheran version of Reformation theology suffered similar abuse. In nineteenth-century Germany, Lutheranism was largely preoccupied with the struggle between liberal and confessional theologians. In spite of considerable internal dissension, they were for the most part, however, in agreement with respect to their understanding of political ethics.[6] The concern for human rights that had been basic to the French Revolution was seen as a threat to the belief in the state as a God-given "order of creation." According to this doctrine, the provision of civil order was seen as government's primary task. The responsibility of the Christian, accordingly, was to serve God and neighbor within the political structures already established rather than to oppose the state as such.

Among the liberals, Friedrich Schliermacher's stress on feeling as the province of religion was given major emphasis. Religion thus became the concern of the inner life. The realm of the church's proper responsibility was the preaching of the Gospel so that faith might be awakened and strengthened in the individual. The "external" or public aspect of life, by contrast, was the responsibility of the "worldly powers," preeminently the state. For public life the law was the primary authority; for personal life, the Gospel. Thus in spite of the formal recognition that ultimately both law and Gospel had their source in the will of God, in practice a clear dualism was created, rigidly separating law from Gospel, public from private life. Luther's complaint that he found it difficult to distinguish properly between law and Gospel had proven groundless. Nineteenth-century theology had discovered a simple solution! Liberals such as Rudolph Sohm and Wilhelm Hermann appealed to the regnant idealism to justify their separation of the political from the spiritual. Sohm could write:

> The gospel frees us from this world, frees us from all questions of this world, frees us inwardly, also from the questions of public life, also from the social question. Christianity has no answer to these questions.[7]

And Hermann was not far behind.

> Once the Christian has understood the moral significance of the state, then he will consider obedience to the government to be his highest vocation within that state. For the authority of the state on the whole, resting as it does upon the authority of the government, is more important than the elimination of any shortcomings which it might have. Should the Christian, due to moral scruples, be unable to carry out his government's command, he will not preach revolution but will gladly suffer the consequences of his disobedience. For the person who is inwardly free, it is more important that the state preserve its historical continuity than that he obtain justice for himself.[8]

It is not difficult to see how these theological legacies, conservative or liberal, would have direct political implications when transplanted to Southern Africa. Whatever the intention of a supposedly apolitical ethic, it inevitably generated specific political consequences. By ignoring the theological legitimacy of the African authorities, the state that serves as an order of creation is in fact the white government, initially German, later British or South African. Any injustice which the Christian might suffer at the hands of this God-given state is to be endured patiently. Opposition is out of the question. The individual is under the Gospel; the state is under the law. Only the former is of the kingdom of God; only the former is the concern of the church. How would this nineteenth-century theological tradition fare when confronting the political realities of the twentieth century? One answer was played out in Europe in the 1930s. Another answer would be given in Africa a generation later.

In Namibia the Rhenish mission had been compelled to assume two arduous tasks throughout its history. By itself, each has been formidable. Together they inevitably generated contradictory imperatives. Like most missionaries of most churches at most periods of history, the German mission saw its primary task that of evangelizing the indigenous population. Its agenda was obvious: a faithful preaching of the Gospel that all may hear the saving word of Christ. In German South West Africa, however, a second obligation fell to the mission. The German colonists, lapsed for the most part from active relationship with the church, were seen as another field of responsibility. German-speaking congregations were founded, and because of the perennial shortage of clergy, missionaries provided the requisite pastoral care. To deny the word of God to either group would be unconscionable. That each group had its own language, needs, and interests was obvious. That those interests might collide was rarely recognized. Like most missionaries, the Germans assumed their own culture to be normative. In working with the German colonists such an assumption was beyond question. What was not seen, however, was the inherent contradiction in this two-fold task. Identification with the fatherland, and in particular, support of the interests of the colonists, could only be obtained at the cost of sacrificing the interests of the indigenous population—unless it could be shown that the purposes of the colonists would somehow advance the well-being of the Africans. Loyalty to the colonists would mean that the mission would be obliged to oppose any attempt by Nama or Herero forces to recover their traditional lands. Such a campaign could only be branded as sinful rebellion. Since the establishment of European civilization in South West Africa would mean the end of any significant African political power, the mission would need to believe that the Africans' interests would be best served by their being mastered by Europeans. This was not usually seen as a loss, since African culture was generally regarded as uncivilized and unworthy of preservation.

By working closely with the colonists the missionaries believed they could be advocates for the Africans, encouraging the Europeans to offer "humane treatment of the native." By influencing the Africans, on the other hand, to develop the virtue of obedience to those in authority, both blacks and whites would be spared bloodshed. Clearly, uprisings by African peoples could only lead to great suffering and final defeat. Obedience was indeed the counsel of wisdom.

A further implication in the mission's support for colonial rule was expressed in its policy of establishing separate ecclesiastical structures for white and black Christians. Long before the imposition of apartheid by South African authorities, the Rhenish mission chose to establish distinct congregations on the basis of race and language. Unlike the Roman Catholics and Anglicans, the mission also created totally separate administrative ministries for blacks and whites at local, regional, and national levels. In practice the mission saw the colonial system as a divinely created polity: the kingdom of God would be effective within it—not against it. Both black and white congregations would develop most fruitfully by cooperating with the policies of whatever government might be in power.

After World War I, Germany's wartime enemy, Great Britain, assumed control of the territory. The mission's support of government policy would now prove no matter of patriotic loyalty for the homeland. Unquestioning support for colonialism continued even when the empire in place had become that of Germany's enemy. Support of British imperialism, as implemented by the Union of South Africa, had become morally correct. The 1915 defeat of the German forces in South West Africa was greeted by the Africans, especially the Herero, as good news. The head of the mission saw it otherwise.

> British propaganda on the subject of liberating nations from the German yoke immediately awakened in many [Herero] . . . a veritable intoxication of freedom. They dreamed of freeing themselves from all bonds with a single blow, as though the Golden Age had already begun. . . . From all over the country, one heard reports of insubordination, rebelliousness, indolence.[9]

The possibility that the Herero might seize the defeat of the Germans as an opportunity for their own liberation was both hoped for and feared. The whites took steps to see that self-determination would not apply for the Namibians. In fact, in the 1920s, South African authorities moved to establish even more rigorous standards for this corner of the British Empire. Steps were taken to restrict freedom of movement by the Namibians and to increase their economic dependence on the whites. The mission acquiesced: the economic viability of the colony and the security of the mission both seemed to demand a renewed emphasis on stability and order. Africans who could see no contradiction between their devotion to the Gospel and their desire for political freedom could find no support for the mission. In the name of avoiding having to deal with politics, it acted to discourage any movement toward local self-determination. Romans 13 was now understood to refer to the British Empire just as previously St. Paul was interpreted to be a defender of the Kaiser. That the powers that be could refer to the political structures of the African peoples was still unthinkable.

A deeper problem obtained. Pietist religion held that Christian responsibility is exhausted in dealing with individual, family, and ecclesiastical matters. Politics lay quite beyond the word of God. To hold, as the Namibian followers of Marcus Garvey did, that Africans are competent to govern themselves, was foolish and could only lead to chaos. The Garvey movement, imported from the United States, had begun to work in Namibia in 1922, much to the consternation of the mission. While its effect was short-lived, the movement demonstrated the persistence of the Herero's repressed desire for political independence. The Rhenish missionary J. Olpp offered a theological interpretation of recent Herero history at the celebration of the silver jubilee of their Windhoek congregation in 1933. His position was representative: the 1904 revolt had been the Herero fall from Eden. Only the Gospel could redeem a people as rebellious as this. The mission had faithfully offered just this solace when the Garvey movement had suddenly intruded, leading the Herero back into sin. Black Christians had returned to the fleshpots of Egypt by believing the false doctrine that salvation consisted in worldly prosperity. The Garveyite doctrine that salvation would include "deliverance from the domination of the white race" was especially noxious and had led to a second fall from grace. Once again, only the mission with its message of a faith that claims to have no connection with socio-political matters can be of any avail.[10]

While the mission was no doubt sincere in its rejection of politics as an appropriate theological concern, its own position was *de facto* highly political and clearly prejudicial to the interests of the people it sought to serve. While the mission regarded itself as being "above politics," its actual policy provided strong support for the British government. Certainly any revolutionary tendencies among the Herero or expatriate "black American agitators" were to be decisively resisted. Thus, the mission found no difficulty in granting Britain the role previously enjoyed by Germany in the old identification of throne and altar. The black members of the church were in both cases consigned to the same apolitical destiny, their traditions and aspirations subservient to a white culture supported by military power. It is clear that nothing as complex and subtle as the reformation doctrine of the two kingdoms was needed to provide the rationale for the mission's continuing sanction of the oppression of the African people. The evidence points to a simpler explanation: theologically and politically unsophisticated pietists unthinkingly acted on the traditional racist assumptions of European culture. Africans were not regarded as possessing sufficient competence to govern themselves, much less a mixed society such as Southern Africa's. Accordingly, for their sake, and for the sake of their superiors, it was argued that God has placed the white man over them as ruler and teacher.

Although marked sympathy and limited support were given the Axis powers by Afrikaners and Germans in Southern Africa during World War II, the victory of the Allies only served to strengthen their own political power. The Union of South Africa, a component of the British Empire, reconstituted itself as a republic in 1961 and also chose to cut its ties to the British Commonwealth. With the exception of some "coloreds," only the whites had the vote, 60 percent of them being Afrikaners. The creation of an Afrikaner-dominated republic would free the nation from British domination. National self-determination based on the principle of "one man, one vote" (for the whites) would guarantee Afrikaner control of the new republic coupled with the opportunity, finally, to reestablish the old vision of a Calvinist, Christian state.

With the establishment of a republic, the churches in Southern Africa began to assume sharply different postures vis à vis the government. A minority of voices in the English-speaking churches—ranging from Anglo Catholic monks to Congregationalist liberals—opposed apartheid as being both politically unjust and a denial of the teachings of Christ. The Afrikaans-speaking churches—typically Calvinist in background—more generally supported the policies of the republic's dominant National party and found that Scripture, especially selected Old Testament texts, required the separation of people as necessary for preserving the Creator's design. White Lutheran clergy, for the most part, attempted to avoid joining the lists of either side, hoping to serve as a bridge between the two groups. Some argued that the Bible neither justifies nor invalidates apartheid. The essential content of the Scriptures is the Gospel of Christ; political issues, such as apartheid policy, must be determined on the basis of secular criteria. Thus, it was argued, a two kingdoms approach to the issue would serve to separate the individual sphere of human life from the political. The former, or spiritual, according to this dualistic interpretation of the doctrine, is the sole responsibility of the church. She cannot claim political competence. The latter is the task of the government which, in imposing discipline and order, saves society from social chaos. The Christian's responsibility with respect to the political order is that of civil obedience. Only if the state specifically prohibits the preaching of the Gospel does obedience to its authority come into question.[11] Thus, both opponents and supporters of apartheid err in seeking to use the Scriptures in defense of their views. Matters of public policy are open to a variety of solutions; the word of God gives no instructions for the design of a Christian society. Neither Afrikaans nor English-speaking church people appear to have found the Lutheran solution persuasive.

After World War II, large, predominantly African churches were created to make it possible to transfer leadership to the indigenous membership. The relation of the new churches to each other and to the numerically small white denominations soon became a critical issue. The traditional mission policy had been based on the European folk church legacy that held that ecclesiastical structures should reflect the differences of language, culture, and ethnicity in any particular area. Expatriate Europeans should be able to continue to worship in their mother tongues just as the new African churches would want to do so. The practical consequence of this policy was to legitimate, if not require, the establishment of an ecclesiastic polity that paralleled the apartheid program of the government. Cultural differences largely shaped by historical factors became the justification for the separation of each ethnic compenent from the others. Some white theologians found no problem with this consequence. They argued that the unity of the church was spiritual, not institutional: unity in Christ does not require organizational union. In practice, the church should structure itself to preserve the identity of each ethnic group so that, among other things, all persons will be free to worship in their own language. A dubious but fateful corollary assumed that separate national church bodies should be established for each ethnic group—the typical practice in American protestantism. Closely connected to this argument was an interpretation of the two kingdoms that emphasized the autonomy of the secular sphere and thus its separation from the Gospel of Christ. The traditional belief, philosophically reinforced by German idealism, that the world of culture generally and the state in particular are "free to follow their own inherent laws of development" without recourse to specifically Christian teaching seems self-evident. The affirmation of the Augsburg Confession, Article VII, that the church is truly present where the Gospel is preached and the sacraments administered was interpreted to mean that it was not necessary to have united churches. It is only necessary that each ethnic group have recourse to the divine word and sacraments.

A second group of theologians, blacks and some whites, sharply disagreed. Their objection was two-fold. They held that church structures both reflect the faith of the church and shape the character of its witness and work. In the Southern African context a radical separation of the essence of the one church from its organizational forms undercuts the authenticity of the Gospel's claim that Christ has brought reconciliation to his people. Segregated ministries of witness and service demonstrate the church's willingness to conform to the world even in the face of blatant social oppression. Thus, far from providing a theological resource for other churches as had been hoped, Lutherans found themselves internally divided over fundamental theological issues in ethics and ecclesiology.

The immediate postwar period would prove critical for the churches in their search for an African identity. Their remarkable growth had by no means been trouble free, especially for the Rhenish mission. The reluctance of the local mission staff to train a black clergy for the church was particularly unfortunate. Their authoritarianism was seen as racially discriminatory. As early as 1926 a group of black lay assistants in the Rhenish mission broke away in protest against white paternalism to form an independent Nama Evangelical Union (Nama Onderwysers en Evangelistebond) at Maltahole. In 1946 the mission actually considered the expedience of turning over its black congregations to the Dutch Reformed Church, which had black clergy of its own, to avoid having to train blacks for the Lutheran ministry. To escape the prospect of having to become a part of the proapartheid Dutch Reformed Church, two thirds of the lay assistants and a third of the total membership seceded from the Rhenish mission to join the African Methodist Episcopal Church, a small mission supported by its black mother church in the United States. Contest over the property of the formerly Rhenish mission congregations proved bitter.

Yet another crisis lay ahead for the mission. Objecting to what it perceived to be the autocratic, colonialist spirit of the white leadership, a group of Herero broke away in August 1955 to organize an independent "Church of the Community" (referred to as the Oruuano), which would be dedicated to minimize its European heritage in favor of a stronger emphasis on African culture. The seriousness of these losses, coupled with increasing pressure from the leadership of the Rhenish mission in Germany, finally led to the establishment of an African church, the Evangelical Lutheran Church (Rhenish Mission), in 1957. The churches that had broken away from the mission declined in influence and numbers largely because of inadequate resources and leadership as well as their inability to appeal to more than a single ethnic group.

In the north, the indigenization of the church was achieved more smoothly. As early as 1927 the Finnish mission had ordained seven Africans and by 1942 there were thirty-one Africans in the ministerium. In 1956 the mission was reconstituted as the Evangelical Lutheran Ovambokavango Church (ELOC). When in 1960 the northern church got its first black bishop, Leonard Auala, an early and heroic leader in the liberation struggle, it became the first major Namibian church to enjoy African leadership. Both of the larger churches now minister to a variety of linguistic and ethnic constituencies. Their cooperation in the establishment of one theological school, Paulinum, laid the critical groundwork for the creation of an anticipated merged church.[12]

The defeat of the Axis powers in World War II evoked expectations of national liberation across Africa. Namibia was no exception. Among the whites, Afrikaner and German sympathy for the Axis powers during the war had been rooted in the belief that if the Allies were defeated, British rule in Southern Africa would come to an end and that an Afrikaner republic could be established in its stead. Among the Africans, the contours of a Namibian liberation movement began to take shape.

Tribal leaders voiced the traditional African resistance to colonialism. Especially vigorous were Herero leaders Hosea Kutako and Chief Fredrick Mahahero who was exiled in neighboring Botswana. In 1946, only after a series of meetings of the Herero advisory councils supported by debates in the reserves and urban locations, Kutako cabled the United Nations. "We want our country to be returned to us. . . . Please let the United Nations be informed again that in South West Africa and Bechuanaland (Botswana) we would like to be under the British Crown; that we deny the incorporation of the country into the Union of South Africa."[13] The Herero were to prove unrelenting in calling the plight of Namibia to the attention of the United Nations. An average of two or three cables were sent to the United Nations each week in 1960. Unable to travel to New York themselves, Maharero and Kutako authorized the Anglican missionary priest, Michael Scott, to represent them at the United Nations. Among the Nama, David Witbooi, son of Hendrik, supported the Herero initiative, thus expressing a new, and increasingly significant spirit of Namibian solidarity. As Witbooi explained to Scott, "The Herero people and I fought many battles against one another. But . . . we now have made peace. Since then and up to today we live as brothers."[14] The tribal leaders' confidence in Scott was understandable. As early as 1948 Scott had preached to a Maharero Day assembly of thousands gathered at Okahandji, "The Hereros' day of liberation is near."[15] As a petitioner for the Herero and Nama he was to appear regularly before the U.N. Trusteeship Committee. His activism earned him the hostility of the white community; his sobriquet: "the political missionary." From his perspective, a church showing no willingness to participate in a moral/political struggle would be irresponsible—even as politics without a moral/religious vision would be unprincipled. Was he not in fact the traditionalist? The interrelatedness of African social institutions, spiritual and political, made for Scott his advocacy of the Namibian cause as legitimate as it was imperative.

Movements to express solidarity among Christian communions became increasingly visible in the postwar years. Throughout the world international ecumenical and confessional bodies were established. In Southern Africa the Federation of Evangelical Lutheran Churches in Southern Africa (FELCSA) was constituted in 1966 by thirteen churches as a forum for pursuing common concerns, especially achieving churchly unity. Significantly, one of the federation's first actions was the planning of a theological conference devoted to an examination of the doctrine of the two kingdoms. For eleven days more than seventy delegates debated the significance of that doctrine in the light of its relevance for Southern Africa. Eleven addresses by a wide variety of South African and European theologians were given. The major outcome of the conference, referred to as the Umpumulo Memorandum after the site of the assembly, the Lutheran Theological College in Umpumulo, Natal, was a stunning public rejection of the South Africa government's apartheid policy. Delegates from virtually all the Lutheran churches in Southern Africa, black and white, claimed that fidelity to the Lutheran understanding of the Gospel required them to break with what had been claimed to be the characteristic tenor of Lutheran political theology, ecclesiastical subservience to the state. Scarcely less startling in academic circles was the basis offered for churchly opposition to the policies of a legitimate, self-proclaimed Christian government. The two kingdoms doctrine, understood in the light of the total sweep of Luther's theology, was claimed to provide the authority needed to mount a consistent and sustained policy of opposition to apartheid. That the doctrine of the two kingdoms had been used by the German Christian party to justify its religious support of Hitler was branded an unconscionable betrayal of the reformation. The Umpumulo Memorandum, a major breakthrough in the churches' long struggle to develop a responsible political theology, was immediately controversial. How was it possible that African churches could interpret the reformation so differently from the understanding common in Europe and North America? How could an apparently abstract academic issue have such explosive practical consequences?

Umpumulo found apartheid, both in practice and theory, to be an inadmissible violation of the word of God in spite of attempts at its theological defense by such participants as P. G. Pakendorf of the Transvaal church. More influential was the address of the rector of the Umpumulo seminary, Gunnar Listerud, which, after review of a variety of criticisms of the two kingdoms theology offered by European theologians, affirmed its validity for the African scene: since both church and state are God's Creation, both are accountable to the law of God. While the state is not a Creation of the Gospel of Christ, it is by no means morally autonomous either. The church, as a bearer of the Word of God, has a "socio-ethical mandate . . . [to] interpret the will of God to the rulers of this world . . . [Indeed], the church cannot only protest and blame when the state has committed an evident injustice, but the church is also entrusted to a positive function to interpret, to educate and to counsel the ruling authorities in the temporal kingdom."[16] In addition to citations from a variety of biblical passages, Listerud made specific reference to Luther's own "socio-political activism" in such essays as "On Secular Authority, to What Extent Should It Be Obeyed," "A Sermon on Keeping the Children in School," and "On War Against the Turk." Listerud concluded his address by a categorical rejection of apartheid on theoretical and practical grounds and called for a policy of racial integration. "This alone would solve the basic problems with which the peoples of this country are faced and bring to fulfillment the demands we have claimed for state and nation building."[17]

The conclusion of the memorandum itself sought to state briefly and clearly the rationale for an activist role for the church on the basis of the two kingdoms doctrine.

The Lutheran teaching of the two kingdoms has given our church freedom to proclaim the gospel of forgiveness of sins and righteousness of God, but it has often been misinterpreted to mean that the church has no responsibility for the state. Temporal government is sometimes understood as an entity in itself with its own laws and ordinances which the citizen must accept in obedience, and it is said as long as the church is allowed to preach the gospel, she has no right to interfere in the temporal government; her task is to preach the gospel of an eternal righteousness of the heart. Having reviewed this doctrine of the two kingdoms biblically and historically, we came to the conclusion that the church has an active and responsible service to the state and society; the church shall protest to the temporal authority when evident injustices have been committed. She is also entrusted with the positive function to interpret and counsel the temporal authorities in terms of the ordinances of creation given for the support and performance of human life, namely: matrimony and family, civil community and culture, state and government. (Apol. XVI). This entails intelligent and responsible political participation on the part of believers.[18]

The memorandum addressed specific political issues as well. Apartheid, the government's grand design for the cultural life of the country, is categorically rejected for political as well as theological reasons.

In its practical implementation, this policy of separate development limits human rights of the non-white citizens as to the right of labor, the right of buying and owning property, the right of free and full education, the right of freedom of speech and of full participation in political and social life. We, therefore, reject the policy of separate development. The main and decisive danger as to the policy of separate development may not be in its practical application but in its ideological orientation and motivation.[19]

In conclusion, the memorandum laments the lack of unity among the Lutheran churches and in the larger ecumenical community. "The disunity of the churches, itself a reflection of traditional prejudice and discrimination, undercuts both the evangelistic and socio-political witness which are essential to the church's own life."[20]

The impact of the newer Luther research on the African church was startling. Not only could the reformation no longer be held responsible for the political passivity of the Lutheran churches, but Luther himself became a resource for the development of a political theology sufficiently resolute to oppose the political establishment. A rethinking of the significance of the two kingdoms for Africa had begun. Once having been used as a justification for obedience to the South African government, the doctrine was being transformed into becoming the basis for challenging that government and for providing a rationale for Christian political activists who seek to build a nonracist democratic future.

Clearly, all in the churches could not have been pleased with the thrust of the Umpumulo Memorandum. It is remarkable that a loosely knit federation, only a year old, would have had the audacity to put its diverse constituency to so difficult a test. Not only did Umpumulo abruptly counter the spirit of apolitical pietism prominent in the churches' history, it signaled a decisive break with the dominant neo-Lutheran romanticism that had so shaped theology that it had become a celebration of the powers of nature and history, and had encouraged belief in preordained, divine laws for society which humanity could discover and respect, but not change. It is not surprising, however, that the conservative President Hahne of the Hermannsburg church felt compelled to voice publicly his disavowal of the Umpumulo statement.

> We beseech the members of our congregations . . . not to expect more from their officials than the service which God has committed to them, namely proclaiming the gospel, administering the sacraments, and providing pastoral care. We encourage all members of our church to place their hope in Jesus Christ alone and not to expect salvation from political programs or earthly powers.[21]

The difficulty the German language congregations had in distinguishing between romantic conservatism with its confidence in the "inherent natural laws" of society and the theology of Luther is understandable, given their strong ethnic loyalties. Nonetheless, in spite of scattered opposition to the Umpumulo Memorandum in the white churches, the federation was not seriously threatened. Indeed, eight years later its four major black churches, with a combined membership of four hundred thousand were able to realize a part of the memorandum's objective by uniting to form the Evangelical Lutheran Church in Southern Africa. The union was clearly understood to be an anti-apartheid act, as it united a variety of black, colored, and Asian groups. When tear gas grenades were thrown into the uniting assembly by anonymous terrorists, the bishops unhesitatingly blamed the South African police.

An even more difficult question, however, remained to be answered. Would any church in Southern Africa actually attempt to implement the political doctrine sketched in the memorandum? It is one thing to say to the membership of the churches that "we reject the policy of separate development." Would any church have the temerity to take the second step and "counsel the temporal authorities" regarding their obligation to establish justice, to recognize their citizens' human rights? When that initiative would come, it would be taken not by missionaries serving white churches or heading African missions, but by the indigenous leadership of the new black churches themselves. It would come from Namibia, from churches historically conditioned to avoid involvement in politics, but now, through the sweep of events, among the most politically engaged of any churches in the world. In Namibia, the churches' protest against the occupation of their country by South African troops is seen as the political consequence of their rejection of apartheid. National independence is regarded as the necessary means for overcoming a particularly bitter colonial experience and its legacy of exploitative racism.

The Open Letter: A New Voice

> South Africa is a Christian country where there is complete freedom of religion. . . . The Gospel is freely preached in Africa in thousands of churches every week. . . . It must, however, be accepted that we will not tolerate people who want to come here to disturb the peace and to undermine law and order. For that we rest our case, amongst others, on the teachings of Luther.
> —J. Weilbach, Private Secretary to South African Prime Minister Vorster, 27 October 1975

On 21 June 1971, the International Court of Justice reversed itself. It surprised the world, and electrified Southern Africa, with the announcement that its 1950 ruling declaring South Africa's mandate to occupy Namibia had been in error; the republic's continued occupation of Namibia was in fact illegal.

The news of the declaration had immediate impact in Namibia. At the Paulinum Seminary a group of students, fresh from a study of Romans 13, was struck by the religious implications of the World Court's announcement. Traditionally, Romans 13 had been used in Southern Africa to justify apartheid. "Let every person be subject to the governing authorities, for there is no authority except from God, and those that exist have been instituted by God (Rom. 13:1)." Did not obedience to the governing authorities have solid biblical support? But now, as one of the students, Zephania Kameeta, would indicate later, ". . . We started for the first time to look at the text within the context of this Southern Africa situation."[22] Romans had held that it is the task of those in authority to reward the good and to punish evil doers. But, in Kameeta's experience,

[u]p to that day in Namibia . . . [governmental] authority was there to punish those who are doing good and to praise those who are doing wrong. And we asked: What's the responsibility of the church in this

kind of situation? Has the church anything to say? Should the church only be concerned about what is to come? Or should the church be the first-taste of the kingdom of God? Should the church keep quiet in view of the suffering of the people, in view of the injustice?[23]

The urgent need to rethink the meaning of Romans 13 in the light of a cultural situation dramatically different from that assumed by Paul was not lost on the students in the school named in his honor. Encouraged by their faculty, especially the German missionary Theo Sundermeier, they began to prepare a formal protest to the prime minister of South Africa, B. J. Vorster. They wished to spell out, in concrete detail, their understanding of what is meant by the Pauline description of the government as "God's servant for good." It had become painfully obvious that the church could not remain silent in the presence of a government that had consistently discriminated against major sections of its own population.

Fortunately, the boards of administration of the two churches supporting Paulinum (one of the few schools in the country open to all ethnic groups) were in session at the time. Bishop Leonard Auala himself, increasingly troubled by reports of human rights violations by the government, was fully sympathetic to the ferment at the seminary. He proposed that the two boards, building on the seminary's document, issue an Open Letter on their own authority. On 30 June 1971 the Open Letter became the official position of the churches themselves.

In remarkably deferential language the letter claimed that the South African government had failed over the years to comply with the U.N. Charter of 1948. The government was now morally obliged to initiate a comprehensive series of fundamental reforms. Seven major criticisms were cited.

- The racial policy of the Republic of South Africa has intimidated the Namibian people, and violated their freedom and safety.
- The Group Areas legislation of the republic has prohibited Namibians from exercising the rights of free movement within their own country.
- South African espionage and intimidation have violated the people's rights to freedom of the press.
- The Namibian people are denied freedom of speech.
- The refusal of the republic to grant voting rights to the black sector of the population has made it impossible for "the indigenous people to work together in a really responsible and democratic manner to build the future" of the nation.

- The Job Reservation Act has effectively broken up family life, "hindered the cohabitation of families" and caused low remuneration and unemployment.
- Most fundamentally, South Africa's imposition of apartheid separates a Namibian people who see themselves as one.

Therefore, the church boards concluded, our "urgent wish is that your government will cooperate with the United Nations, . . . and will see to it that the Human Rights [charter] be put into operation, that South West Africa may become a self-sufficient and independent state."[24]

A more fundamental act of opposition to the government could not be imagined. The white community in South Africa and Namibia was shocked. It had taken for granted that Namibia's blacks were content to live under the authority of Pretoria. The general public in both countries was astonished to learn that conservative evangelical black churches would (1) choose to become politically engaged at all, and (2) presume to fault the republic for failure to comply with the standards of an international political organization of which it was a member.

Along with copies of the Open Letter, the boards of the two churches sent, on the same day, a Letter to the Congregations explaining their action. The boards carefully indicated the rationale for the churches' public protest. They pointed out that the World Court a week earlier had declared South Africa's occupation of Namibia to be illegal: the republic's mandate had indeed expired; Namibia had become the political responsibility of the United Nations. The claim by the republic at the World Court that Namibia was being peaceably ruled was clearly false. The imposition of apartheid had increasingly generated fear and hatred among the population as a whole. The so-called peace that the government claimed to have maintained had been enforced by a denial of freedom of assembly in general and had necessarily restricted the church's freedom to spread the Gospel. Laity and clergy of different ethnic groups had been regularly prevented from assembly for worship. Thus the very unity of the church was being violated by the government in its prohibition of multiracial congregations. The church was also concerned to speak for more than its own welfare. It charged that the insistence by the republic that self-government and independence for the African peoples could be permitted only if the indigenous groups were kept in separate, geographically confined homelands had both isolated the Africans and effectively denied them the opportunity to participate in the development of their own country.[25]

The Open Letter and the Letter to the Congregations served unmistakable notice that a new day had dawned. Both documents quickly achieved a kind of unofficial confessional status in the Namibian churches. The indigenous churches had found their voice. They were now prepared to speak to their own people, and to the highest levels of government, with an authority and a freedom previously unknown.

In recent years an official publication of the Evangelical Lutheran Church in SWA/Namibia (Rhenish Mission) underscored the significance of this new profile.

The Evangelical Lutheran Church had for years maintained a posture of "obedience to the divinely ordained authority" [of the government] which it had inherited from the early missionaries. The socio-political situation in Namibia, however, increasingly demanded a clear and un-equivocal stand from the church on the issues of human rights, freedom and national independence.[26]

It is that "however" that marks a major transformation in theology and ethics—especially among the Lutheran churches. The Open Letter and the supporting pastoral Letter to the Congregations served notice that a fundamental shift in consciousness had oc-curred. Given their transformative implications, it is striking that formally the letters rest not on a specific evangelical locus, but on the traditional reformation insistence that it is the church's obliga-tion "to preach the law to the prince." No uniquely theological argument is proposed. The churches assume that they have a duty to proclaim God's law to all. To ignore the prince, or, in this case, the prime minister, is theologically irresponsible. Significantly, the churches did not believe it necessary to press biblical language onto the government. Nonetheless, while eschewing technical theologi-cal argument, the churches were not willing to allow that the people's demand for justice and equity is also dispensable. The churches clearly spoke from a conviction that the imperative for justice rests on a divine mandate. They also assumed, perhaps too optimistically, that the government would recognize that its own authority is not self-derived, but prehends from a standard of justice that transcends its positive legal code. That the churches have the responsibility and competence to spell out concrete requirements for justice is simply presupposed, however unprecedented it must have seemed in Namibia. Where the missionary tradition had per-mitted the theology of the Reformation to decay by ignoring the reign of God in the social structures of civil justice and public order, the Namibian churches, under Namibian leadership, found their way through to affirm his purposes in both the community of Christ and society as a whole.

The churches' two letters provoked a storm of controversy. Some white clergy charged that the Namibian leadership had abandoned their pastoral responsibilities for the sake of political engagement. Others countered that the familiar restriction of the Word of God to purely spiritual concerns in contrast to worldly matters is neither biblically based nor pastorally responsible. The churches' own view was that they needed to identify themselves with "the downtrodden masses yearning for liberation as well as serve as the conscience of the nation."[27]

With a single stroke, the churches had begun to prepare the way for a grafting of liberation theology's commitment for solidarity with the oppressed onto their Reformation tradition. Theologically, the churches had attempted to retrive a neglected element in that legacy: the preaching of law and Gospel as a judgment and a mercy for all. But that such a divine word would have the power to bring both promise to oppressed Namibians and condemnation to their oppressors was startlingly new.

Having found their voice in 1971, the churches have become increasingly committed to the struggle for independence. The Anglican church had been first to be openly critical of the government—a natural extension of the minority anti-apartheid movement within South African Anglicanism.[28] Lutherans and Roman Catholics had been slower to challenge the government publicly. But after the Lutheran initiatives in 1971 were quickly supported by Anglicans and Catholics, these three churches became particularly active in defending victims of political oppression. The churches were the first to make the general public aware of the floggings administered by progovernment tribal leaders after the 1973 elections. Probably it was only because of sustained church pressure that the courts were finally compelled to deal with the issue: floggings were legally prohibited in 1975.

The churches have also chosen to be defenders of detainees who have claimed to have been tortured at the hands of South African military forces. On 30 April 1973, the Lutheran bishops submitted a list of thirty-seven names to South African Prime Minister Vorster. The charge: the people named were willing to risk testifying in court that they had been tortured by South African police. The response, after three months: the prime minister simply denied the truth of the charges. There would be no investigation. Undaunted, the churches pressed their accusation again and in May 1977 charged that the torture of Namibian detainees had now become "standard practice" by South African police.[29]

Particularly revealing was the report, *The Green and the Dry Wood*, published by two priests of the Oblates of Mary Immaculate in January 1983, which provided detailed documentation of human rights violations and torture for the decade 1971–81. The government's response was to ban the publication and to expel its authors from the country.

The persecution of the churches by the South African government goes largely unnoticed overseas. Internally, the churches' advocacy of the oppressed has extracted its price. Since a large number of the white church leaders are from abroad, the government has found it easy to expel critics who embarrass local authorities. Thus, successive Anglican bishops, Colin Winter in 1972 and Richard Wood in 1975, were deported to their native England. Particularly outspoken in giving vigorous ecumenical support to the 1971 Open Letter, Winter had also championed a group of African strikers when they were brought to trial in 1972, while Wood had been equally zealous in his exposé of South African flogging of SWAPO members in 1974. The current bishop, James Kauluma, as a Namibian, cannot be dispensed with as easily, even though he is no less uncompromising in his opposition to apartheid. The persecution of the church continues with no sign of abatement, but so far it has proven counterproductive. When the church becomes a victim of attack, its credibility in the eyes of the African community can only grow.[30]

The initiative represented by the Open Letters has proven widely influential in Namibia's ecumenical community. The Council of Churches in Namibia, within which the large black communions play a major role, issued a series of official statements of its own that flesh out the assumptions and substance of the 1971 letters.[31] Three in particular can be cited.

In January 1983 a new Open Letter to the South African prime minister had as its burden the appeal to "act now to see that the United Nations Security Council Resolution 435 is implemented without delay."[32] The churches argued that their "commitment to reconciliation, justice, peace, and the preservation of human life" compelled them to urge the granting of independence to Namibia "as the only just and concrete solution to our country's plight."[33] The postponement of independence for Namibia because of the Cuban presence in Angola was interpreted as "a deliberate act of obstruction." Vigorous exception was also taken to the "regime of Draconian laws, proclamations and amendments" enforced by the

South African administrator general in Namibia; particularly condemned was the government's policy of arresting and jailing citizens without charge or trial. Finally, the "brutal and unprovoked attacks on innocent people" by the military was understood to be aimed specifically at "silencing the witness of the church in Namibia."[34] Broad ecumenical support for the argument of the 1971 Open Letter clearly had been attained.

A year after its Open Letter to the prime minister, the Council of Churches of Namibia issued an Open Letter to the European and North American churches.[35] The council regarded it necessary to anticipate the public attention the new South African prime minister, P. W. Botha, would receive during his proposed visit to selected European capitals. The thrust of this letter, too, addressed fundamental issues of justice. The ten signatories, claiming to represent over 80 percent of the country's population, emphasized three areas of concern.

- Politically, the churches charged that "South Africa has turned the whole nation into a military camp."[36]
- Economically, they claimed that the continued occupation of the country by South Africa has served only to enhance the wealth of foreign companies while "the ordinary Namibian" is denied a rightful share in the wealth of the land. The South African insistence upon the establishment of separate ethnic governments, an essential feature of apartheid, has proven both wasteful and corrupt.
- Socially, the council argued that the polarization between whites and blacks as presented by the government-controlled radio and television and the strictly censored press has only served to exacerbate racial tensions. Particularly objectionable has been the government's policy of encouraging a "growing paranoia" by inculcating a fear of the indigenous population among the children in its white schools.

Whatever the merits of its argument, this Open Letter to the Churches evoked only limited response.

Seizing the opportunity offered by the visit of Senator Edward Kennedy to Namibia in January 1985, the eight member churches of the Council of Churches welcomed him and his party "in the name of our living God to whom all praise is due."[37] An ecumenical delegation of twelve church leaders called to his attention a series of abuses in the belief that the U.S. Congress will continue to play a major role in determining Namibia's fate. The American linkage of the Cuban presence in Angola to a settlement for Namibian independence was rejected once more. The delegation was particularly critical of the republic's educational policy: South Africa remains unwilling to permit the Namibian people to prepare to assume responsibility for self-government. The statement did not hesitate to protest "the blocking of the implementation of the United Nations Resolution 435 by the South African government with the direct connivance of the present government in Washington."[38] And yet the delegation's final word was a wistful plea: the churches look to the United States for assistance in their country's "peaceful movement to independence." Whether the U.S. political system will prove to be more responsive to Namibian appeals than has South Africa remains to be seen.

The vigorous and articulate role played by the churches in their new political activism raises a host of questions. Will not the highly controversial character of religiously based social criticism prove divisive for the churches? Serious strain between whites and blacks within particular communions can be cited.[39] On the other hand, churches that represent a very wide range of doctrine and order have found fundamental consensus both in their assessment of their country's plight, and in concrete proposals for an alternate political dispensation. This body of agreement achieved by the churches across old ecclesiastical barriers is a remarkable achievement.

Within the Lutheran community the Letters of 1971 raised the most fundamental theological questions. Karl Barth's well-known criticism of Lutheranism's passivity in the face of German nationalism was not entirely irrelevant to Southern Africa.[40] White congregations in Namibia and South Africa, for the most part German speaking, took strong exception to the black churches' presumption of competence to criticize national policy. Did not the pietism that shaped the religious consciousness of both black and white congregations in Southern Africa rule out a consideration of any but strictly "spiritual" matters as having Christian value? Did not the doctrine of the two kingdoms require the church to be silent, or at least, exceedingly reserved, in the face of controversial political issues? Landesprobst K. Kirschnereit, head of the small but influential German Evangelical Lutheran Church in South West Africa, developed an elaborate theological rationale for silence.

Should it be impossible for the church to give either an unqualified Yes or an unqualified No [in the face of apartheid], then she has to remain silent. Her proclamation dare not bind the consciences of her members or burden them with one-sided advice. Of course, the church's silence with respect to definite concrete problems is at the same time a form of speaking. This silence transfers the responsibility for decisions which must be made away from the church and onto the shoulders of the responsible, mature citizens, both Christian and non-Christian. Thus the church removes the problem of "separate development" from consideration as a question of faith requiring a theological answer and restores it to the competence of the politicians, who must render a decision on the basis of factual considerations and in responsibility for their own consciences.[41]

What would be the basis for the selection of the pertinent "facts" and what would be the criteria that would inform conscience were not pursued. Instead, it is an interpretation of the doctrine of the two kingdoms that had been rejected at Umpumulo that was once more pressed into service. To be sure it is not the purpose of that doctrine "that the state and its political life [be] turned over to their own autonomous laws.[42] Nor is it claimed that in the kingdom of the left hand God "does not rule at all but has withdrawn, as it were, from the field." Rather, "the doctrine of the two kingdoms merely wishes to differentiate between the ways in which God rules while providing a cogent theological explanation for such a distinction; but it does not give the slightest cause for concluding that God does not rule at all in the world."[43]

A policy of silence regarding political matters is, however, supposedly biblically based.

The guiding principle that one ought to keep silent where the Holy Scriptures do not speak must be revived again in the church so that she does not become a forum for solving all the world's problems. But when the church keeps silent about questions directly related to her proclamation, this is not to say that she abandons the world to its own devices. On the contrary she restores the right to decide to her members who must live out their lives as citizens. . . .[44]

The fact that the majority of the people of the country, and an even greater portion of the church are not permitted to live as citizens drops from sight. The church, in this perspective, has no responsibility for public affairs. "The church is no agency for the criticism of public affairs, and her proclamation cannot be a moralistic drumbeat for the alleviation of abuses for which she is unable to claim responsibility."[45] In sum, "[w]hen the church knows how a matter concerns her, she speaks; when the way in which a matter affects the church remains unclear, she is better advised to keep silent."[46]

The philosophical basis for Kirschnereit's views, since repudi-

ated by the leadership of his church, were not at that time altogether unrepresentative.

> No one in South West Africa thinks that "separate development"
> [apartheid] is heaven on earth, not the government and not even the
> membership of the German Evangelical Lutheran Church. But to con-
> sider "separate development" as something absolutely evil in itself can
> be done only with the help of a preconceived ideology. The only
> reproach that can be lodged against the German Evangelical Lutheran
> Church is that it does not share this ideology.[47]

Thus, the head of a Namibian church did not hesitate to use the
media to announce his theological rationale for silence even while
arguing there should be no churchly opposition to apartheid.

A quite different interpretation of the church's silence was offered by Pastor Albertus Maasdorf.

> Whenever [the black church] has anything to say to the whites, we
> [blacks] always must hear the judgment: "Whatever she says is stupid
> and irrelevant!" That is why it is so important that both the state and the
> white population understand that it may so please God to make use of
> the blacks today in order to say: "Thus says the Lord." God's criticism
> against the white man and his system can also be spoken out of a black
> mouth. That is why I have said that it is a difficult task for the church.
> And it can be that this is an obligation which demands too much from
> the church as she is and as she exists among the blacks. Perhaps this has
> been just the reason why the church so often in the past has elected to
> take a neutral position. It can be that just because she fears to say a
> word that the church will opt once more to become a still and a silent
> church."[48]

Silence, however, would not prove an adequate response. The Open
Letter had broadcast seeds that would soon bear rich fruit.

Swakopmund: An African Appeal

The setting seemed a fantasy: a charming yellow and white baroque church flanked by palms, its ornate bell tower topped by the
clocks, double onion dome, and cross, typical of Bavaria. But on a
warm summer day in February 1975, representatives of twelve
African judicatories gathered in the church in Swakopmund on the
Namibian coast to hammer out a definitive response to the questions generated by the new activism.[49] Clearly, a new situation

demanded a new response. The witness of the church in the apartheid controversy could not be one of silence. Does the doctrine of the two kingdoms, however, inhibit political theology or validate it? Was the turmoil created by the Open Letter due only to its sheer novelty? Or was it simply theologically immature?

After two and a half days of intense debate the churches were able to reach a remarkable consensus. Their declaration, "Appeal to Lutheran Christians in Southern Africa Concerning the Unity and Witness of Lutheran Churches and their Members,"[50] was an unqualified endorsement of the witness of the Open Letter. A. W. Habelgaarn, president of the Federation of Evangelical Lutheran Churches in Southern Africa, publisher of the appeal, declared the document to be "the most important ever issued by our Federation."[51] In effect, the churches in Southern Africa, including the three in Namibia, had prepared a new confession of faith, occasioned by a new historical crisis. African clergy and laity, with significant support from a younger generation of missionaries and consultants representing the Lutheran World Federation, found here an opportunity to support the original Namibian protest and to develop its implications.

Since the two kingdoms doctrine had been used by the churches to legitimate their tacit support for Southern Africa's racist tradition, the appeal began with an act of theological self-criticism. Repentance as well as promise would be required. The appeal frankly acknowledged the presence of "alien principles" in the churches' traditional theology, beliefs that have come to threaten their faith and to destroy their unity in doctrine, witness, and practice.[52] The most noxious of these dangerous beliefs were summoned for exposure and repudiation:

- the pervasive belief that loyalty to one's ethnic group requires one to worship in a church that is "dependent on birth or race or ethnic affinities";
- the insistence that the churches, out of loyalty to the past, must remain divided on the basis of ethnic differences and thus give explicit support to apartheid;
- the belief that the unity of the church is "a spiritual unity only" and therefore does not need to be manifested in corporate life;
- the belief that "the political and economic system[s] of our country are to be shaped according to natural laws only, inherent in creation or merely according to considerations of practical expediency, without being exposed to the criterion of God's love as revealed in the biblical message."

While the positive affirmations of the appeal were divided into nine articles, the confession had but two foci, ecclesiology and ethics, both being grounded in justification by faith. Justification was given primacy of place both to stress the continuity of this new confession with the classical theological symbols, as well as to demonstrate that in our time justification has consequences for both church and society and this is incompatible with the philosophy and institutions of apartheid. Accordingly, the "full mutual acceptance of all is . . . our answer to God's grace, leading to full participation in society." The familiar criticism that Lutheran theology generally has not been sufficiently strong in ecclesiology and ethics appears to be acknowledged, for the burden of the appeal is to address both of these fronts with special attention.

Justification by faith discloses the church to be that community into which entry depends not on birth or race or natural affinities, but solely on the call of God, confessed in faith and bestowed in baptism. As the body of Christ, the church is thus literally "supernatural," and has as its essential task that of clearly showing its God-given unity. "Differences of race, language, customs and traditions are given by God for the enrichment of the church: and may not be misused to serve as a justification for division among Christians." The appeal thus declares, in a direct repudiation of apartheid, that "all nations, races, cultures and traditions are called and assembled to be the one people of God, to which they all belong together in one and the same way." The church's unity is not characterized by an ethnic uniformity displayed in its congregations, but to the contrary, by the very diversity of the people of God gathered up into the one Christ.

This vigorous emphasis on the visible unity of the church is both a critique of parish, regional, and national structures, and a criterion for their reform. It is also a repudiation of the conventional pietist notion that the institutional aspects of church life are of only secondary importance, that juridical considerations are irrelevant to the Gospel. Significantly, it was the German church in Namibia that proposed grounding the church's visible unity in its sacramental life: in baptism, all Christians, irrespective of race, are made members of the one church. In the preaching of the Gospel and the celebration of the Sacrament of the Altar, the faithful share in the fellowship of all believers. To exclude laity or clergy from participation in the means of grace on the basis of racial factors serves actually to destroy both the ministerial office, and the unity of the church itself.

Finally, ecclesiology implies mission. And the mission of the church to preach the Gospel of reconciliation compels the Christian community to struggle against all oppressive structures and conditions, the most prominent of which being, of course, legalized racism. Reconciliation was not minimized at Swakopmund. However diminished its significance has come to be held elsewhere, in Africa reconciliation is seen as an essential, fundamental, counter-cultural dynamic. It demonstrates unmistakably a subversion of the structures of apartheid and projects a positive alternative rooted in the Gospel of justification. As a visible exemplar of a unity inclusive of all races, the church makes its most profound witness to a society permeated by racial hostility. To fail to take seriously its mission to manifest a visible unity rooted in the Gospel is to abandon the promise of the Gospel itself.

It is hardly surprising that the brave words of Swakopmund were not immediately implemented in the congregations and regional churches. But a fundamental theological decision had been made there, and there could be no retreat from it in church teaching in the future. The Africans had placed the church itself at the center of their witness and had called it to a reformation as radical as any it had ever known.

The appeal found that justification by faith has wide-reaching ethical implications, several of which represent a sharp break with much traditional practice. The recognition that Christ justifies sinners implies that they who receive his acceptance are obliged to accept each other as unconditionally as he has accepted them. Furthermore, this evangelical righteousness is the criterion not only of personal, but of social relationships. It had never been doubted that individual Christians should forgive as they have been forgiven. But that this acceptance has social implications could only have seemed, in Africa, to be an innovation. The appeal indicates three of them.

- The church is mandated by Christ to speak not only to the conscience of Christians, but directly to the government as well. It is called to be a watchman warning of imminent disaster (Ezekiel 33) as well as a shepherd tending his flock (John 10). To continue to avoid addressing clamant social ills is an act of irresponsibility before God.
- As justification is a gift, so creation too is a gift. It is God as Creator who authenticates the dignity of the human personality. Thus when a governmental authority presumes to violate any

individual's God-given dignity, it must be steadfastly resisted. The government's abusive treatment of persons of color demands divine censure.

• The church's critique does not rest content with generalities. The specific political structures that abuse human beings are to be identified and rejected. "We are convinced that this whole system needs to be radically reconsidered and reappraised in the light of the biblical revelation and the general experiences of mankind." The reformation's classic appeal to the authority of both the word of God and to reason finds startling confirmation.

Swakopmund, baroque transplant on the Namibian coast, would prove to send tremors through the global Lutheran community. It made apartheid forever an unavoidable theological issue. The Lutheran World Federation assembly in Dar es Salaam, Tanzania, but two years later, building on the momentum of Swakopmund, would hold that since "confessional integrity" requires "concrete manifestations of unity in worship and in working together," apartheid is a repudiation of confessionalism.[53]

A *status confessionis* was declared to exist calling all churches in Southern Africa "publicly and unequivocally [to] reject the existing apartheid system."[54] Traditionally Lutheranism had understood confessional integrity to refer to purity of doctrine. Africa had led the church to identify ethical fidelity to the Gospel of equal importance. Justification is by faith. But since faith is unitive, racism is heresy.

The Emerging Focus: Ecclesiology

While the ethical witness of the Namibian church is consciously derived from the biblical tradition as mediated by German and Finnish pietism, within the last two decades a specifically African temper has become increasingly obvious. The Namibian theological riddle: "How can pietism generate political activism?" has found an answer. North European pietism transplanted to a radically different cultural setting has the power to develop strengths unknown in the lands of its origin. Conversely, a new social context can transform pietism by giving it new cultural resonance. In Southern Africa the politically ambiguous character of pietism has become resolved: the Christian gospel can indeed generate holistic political commitment. Similarly, the privatistic preoccupation of the Protestant tradition can be overcome in favor of a vigorous new sense of the centrality of the church for Christian life and witness. Reflection on the sequence by which an authentically Namibian ethic has emerged is instructive.

POLITICAL THEOLOGY AS THE OCCASION FOR EVANGELICAL RENEWAL

It is difficult to say which is the most surprising: that a group of theological students would be able to reverse the traditional understanding of a key biblical text—or that their arguments would prove sufficiently persuasive to win the immediate assent of the highest levels of authority in their churches—or that that interpretation would quickly prove the basis for the church's repudiation of the government's claim to moral competence. That Romans 13 has figured prominently in traditional attempts to enlist the church on the side of the status quo is well-known. A simple reading of the text might appear to allow for no other option. The Paulinum students' interpretation that stressed the governing authority's mandate to be a servant for the good of the people is, however, as irrefutable as it is novel. The declaration of the World Court that the *de facto* government of Namibia is illegitimate was, unfortunately, a bloodless abstraction that has, for the most part, been ignored in practice by the Western democracies. But the churches' claim, in behalf of the majority of the people of the country, that the government is incompetent, that it has consistently failed to fulfill its obligations before God and the nation, is quite another matter. Not only has the church presumed to enter the political fray as a fully qualified participant, she has clearly signaled the people's denial of the government its sources of authority, the uncoerced assent of the governed. As a sign of its own political responsibility, the churches have published, time after time, carefully detailed memorandums calling attention to concrete abuses of civil rights by the political authorities as well as equally specific citations of the reforms that the people seek. This willingness to be concrete is both a measure of the Namibian churches' willingness to take risks and a demonstration of their total commitment to their political task. Political theology has not been merely an option for the churches. It has become a basic and inescapable part of its responsibility as shepherd and watchman.

THE PULSE OF ECCLESIOLOGY: THE UNITY OF CHRISTIANS

Chronologically, the new Namibian ethical witness began with a political critique. Very quickly, and without abandoning that political commitment, the churches demonstrated how their concern for the health of the nation's social existence was actually rooted in the Gospel itself, especially in the social form of the Gospel as expressed in the church's own life as community. When the government used both secular and religious arguments to separate the people of the country into different groups on the basis of race, the church found the Gospel obligated it to protest. From the perspective of the Gospel, the separation of persons into different churches on the basis of ethnic distinctions, makes a travesty of the cross. The good news that the alienation between God and humanity, and the estrangements within humankind, have been overcome through the death of Jesus Christ, is made of no effect in a society confined by apartheid. The churches' indefatigable opposition to legally enforced racism is not a meddling in secular affairs beyond its realm of responsibility. Rather, the unity of the body of Christ can tolerate no imposition of barriers that would prevent the baptized from sharing in their life of common worship.

That racism flourishes in today's world, especially it seems in those parts of Africa most affected by European culture, is unmistakable. But that such racism can be elevated to a legal principle that prohibits the body of Christ from obeying its Lord's command that its followers love one another as he has loved them can only be rejected as a blatant attack on the church's own reason for being. The intensity of the church's insistence on the freedom to express its own unity can be understood negatively as a rejection of traditional South African culture. Its positive roots are far deeper, however, and should not be minimized. In addition to the pervasive emphasis on the church's unity within the New Testament, a more recent voice has also been influential.

When the appeal was being drafted as Swakopmund, the Germans from the old Rhenish mission, itself headquartered in Barmen, were alert to the remarkable similarity between the church's plight in contemporary Southern Africa, and that of the confessing church in Germany during the Nazi period.[55] Representatives of Lutheran, Reformed, and Union churches had gathered at Barmen in late May 1934 to formulate an ecumenical response to the increasing domination of the Protestant churches by the Nazi regime. The churches believed themselves to be in a *status confessionis,* a time of crisis requiring a decision either for the freedom of the church to confess Christ without political compromise, or for an acquiescence to a takeover by the Nazi authorities. Among the six theses affirmed at Barmen, the third would prove particularly influential for the drafters of the Swakopmund Appeal.

Speaking the truth in love, we are to grow up in every way unto him who is the head, unto Christ, in whom the whole body is knit together." Ephesians 4:15f.

The Christian church is the congregation of brothers in which Jesus Christ acts today as the Lord, in Word and Sacrament, through the Holy Spirit. It has to witness as the church of forgiven sinners in the midst of a sinful world with its faith as with its obedience, with its message as with its order, that it is his possession alone, and while waiting for his coming it lives and wants to live by his guidance and succor. We reject the false teaching that the church may be permitted to abandon the substance of its message and its order at its own pleasure or that it may exchange them for the world views and political convictions that are currently dominant.[56]

At Barmen it had been clear that the confessing church did not have the liberty to tailor its teachings and structure to conform to the ideology of the Nazi Reich. A generation later, delegates at Swakopmund, hosted by a church founded by a Barmen-based mission, would not fail to see the ominous parallel. Once again, an evangelical church was called to decide whether its future would lie in adapting its faith and order to conform to a powerful racist state, or in remaining true to its crucified Lord, the head of a community of forgiven sinners. Once again it found itself thrust into crisis. Again, a *status confessionis* had emerged. The church could not ignore the specifically religious character of apartheid that in principle defies the church's claim that Christ is Lord.

The African experience would come to echo the German in yet another way as well. In dealing with a totalitarian state it became imperative to recognize that neither order nor faith dare be compromised. Justification by faith is no private possession generated by the believer's subjectivity. To the contrary, it is the good news entrusted to the church for the healing of the nations. It is the message that binds believers to a unity more profound than that of race or nation. The freedom of the church to express that unity by visibly celebrating the inclusiveness of the company of the redeemed is not only a doctrinal issue. It is the criterion by which the governing structures of the church itself are to be judged. The order of the church, no less than its confession of faith, must witness to the church's openness to all.

ECCLESIOLOGY AS PARTICIPATION IN SUFFERING

The Namibian church's identification with "the downtrodden masses yearning for liberation," is a remarkable demonstration of the indigenization of the Gospel in Africa. The churches have committed themselves to a breathtakingly difficult task: the shaping of a new national identity, one that will destroy the basic social fact of the nation's history—the segregation of its ethnic groups at the expense of the indigenous population. The contradiction between inherited social structures and an alternate vision of Namibian identity affects every aspect of the churches' life today.

The most important of the liberation movements working for independence is SWAPO which, in fact, is a legally recognized, if relentlessly harassed, political party. Popular support for SWAPO, especially in the Christian community, is massive. In any free election it would doubtless prove victorious. So-called external SWAPO, based in Angola, and active within Namibia as an underground insurgency force, is the prime opponent to the government's forces. South Africa's effort to maintain control of its one-time mandate in the face of SWAPO pressure has led it to effect a general militarization of the country. Three units are presently active: the South African Defense Force (the occupation army of the Republic of South Africa), the South West African Territorial Force (the Namibian military) and Koevoet (Afrikaans for "crowbar"), an agency of the Namibian secret police. Some 50,000 South Africans and an undisclosed number of Namibians are deployed in these units. As voluntary enlistments proved inadequate, conscription of blacks was begun in 1979. Namibians from age 16 to 25 are subject to call. The churches have repeatedly protested against the draft as it compels Namibians to fight against members of their own family who may be active in SWAPO. As the draft continues, thousands of men and boys have fled the country to avoid conscription; at conservative estimate, some 10 percent of the population is now in exile.

The Namibians are particularly fearful of Koevoet, which they consider a terrorist organization. For example, church people charge that Koevoet uses captured SWAPO uniforms and arms to entrap persons suspected of being sympathetic to SWAPO. Thus, while South Africa blames SWAPO for the bombing of the Ondangua Post Office in late 1984 that resulted in two fatalities and a number of wounded, the local population holds Koevoet responsible.

Perhaps it is understandable that it is the churches that receive a major brunt of military harassment. Since they provide a broadly inclusive national structure not under the control of the government, they are rightly seen as constituting a massive grass roots threat to South African control. Congregations complain that their churches are being destroyed by government troops. A bishop speaks of churches that have been pressed into service for military purposes, complete with "Kill SWAPO" graffiti. In at least one case a Lutheran church was turned into a latrine. Bishop Kleopas Dumeni has given a graphic description of the interruption of worship services at Elombe in May 1982. After the congregation of some 650 had been ordered out of the church by the soldiers, the pastors separated from the laity, these events occurred.

> The soldiers checked out all women and children and ordered them to sit down at a separate place. All men were assembled at the main entrance of the church. They were then taken by the soldiers one by one in order to be interrogated and beaten. Some of the women started to cry, when they saw that the men were really badly beaten. The soldiers then ordered the men to move further behind the walls of the church building. [The women] too were beaten and kicked with boots. . . . After they had finished beating up people, the soldiers left. . . . In spite of the fact that the worship service was disturbed, and men tortured, the soldiers left without catching SWAPO whom they reportedly were looking for inside the church.[57]

The printing press at Oniipa, sole publisher of materials in the Ovambo language, has been bombed twice and rebuilt twice. Anglicans have witnessed the destruction of hospitals, churches, and schools in addition to the bombing of their seminary and diocesan buildings at Odibo. In all of these cases the local people hold the government forces culpable.

An extensive survey documenting the use of torture by the government was published by Roman Catholic authorities in 1978.[58] One item cites twenty-five Namibians who died mysteriously while being detained by the government. The author of the report, Heinz Hunke, provincial for the Oblates of the Immaculate Heart of Mary, was subsequently expelled from the country. Since then, church officials have continued to protest their clergy and laity being jailed and subjected to physical and psychological abuse. In 1983, Dennis Hurley, Roman Catholic archbishop of Durban, publicly charged Koevoet with a series of illegal acts of violence. The South African authorities responded by indicting him for violating laws that forbid criticism of the police. Two years later the charges were dropped, probably because a public trial would inevitably have called international attention to the substance of his accusations.[59]

The bombings of the church's press, the destruction of schools and churches, terrorist attacks on the headquarters of the Council of Churches in Namibia, and the arbitrary imprisonment of pastors and lay leaders without trial, have become routine. Persecution is the price to be paid when a church dares to champion justice in an unjust land. It has also proven to be a discipline that strengthens the resolve of the oppressed, and, particularly in this case, a sign of solidarity between the churches and the great bulk of the population.

Appropriately, the theological significance of persecution had also been recalled at Swakopmund. Luther's essay of 1539, "The Councils and the Church," had suddenly become salient. In rejecting the notion that the treasures of the church were its relics, the reformer cited "seven marks" as the real signs of the church's authenticity. In addition to the classic emphasis on the preached Word and the sacraments of Baptism and the Eucharist, Luther added four others: the public forgiveness of sins (absolution), the ordained ministry, public worship, and the persecution of Christians. A church that is in tension with the culture of which it is a part, will need to expect persecution. In Namibia the rediscovery of suffering as a mark of a faithful church has served to strengthen its biblical and evangelical foundations.

ECCLESIOLOGY AS THE SIGN OF RECONCILIATION

Reconciliation has not been a prominent theme in Western theological ethics in recent years. Nor does it figure prominently in most versions of liberation theology. In Namibia it is fundamental.[60] The emphasis on reconciliation in the appeal has proven to be no mere formality. If the church is to be a credible advocate for inclusiveness, it can endorse neither the old tribalism nor the new racism. The struggle for an independent nation has created special problems for a church that seeks to encompass the concerns of all its people. Bishop Kleopas Dumeni has been candid.

> We must remember that the church is the church, not a political party. We must serve all people including all parties and all points of view. Now this is not easy when SWAPO people and government informers belong to the same parish and come to the same pastor. But we must serve everyone. Truth, justice, and peace must be the same for all. Our message is the gospel of reconciliation.[61]

Inclusiveness does not imply permissiveness. He continued:

> When we see that an informer is collaborating with the South African authorities we make clear, "You are a part of the killing. If you are an informer, and you give information, you are responsible"[62]

In the future, reconciliation will be even more urgent for the church, according to Dumeni.

When our thousands of exiles are free to return, they will come home with many different views. Our future problem then will not be communism. It will be reconciliation. How can we become one people when this long period of suffering has forced so many of us into exile? Yet we will need to find a way to come together.[63]

The growth and renewal of the church continue, even under incredible pressure. Its most significant discovery in its time of testing has been the new and deepened sense of its mission: its political action, its unity and suffering and work of reconciliation combine not so much to describe a new agenda, as to reveal with fresh clarity what it means to be the church. It is not only a bearer of good news in a dangerous world. It is more than that. The church is itself the actualization of the good news: human beings can live lives of reconciliation, in solidarity, under the cross, even while addressing the most urgent moral abuses of their time.

The Africanization of the Two Kingdoms

In Africa, as in Europe, the reformation doctrine of the two kingdoms has been the subject of intense theological debate. Some have held that this doctrine is a theological dead end, lacking adequate biblical support, and leading inevitably to Christian social irresponsibility. Others have argued that while the doctrine has biblical roots and represents a summary of Luther's social ethic, it is exceedingly difficult to use today in societies so markedly different from the late medieval Europe the reformers addressed. Still others have held that the doctrine, while capable of being distorted, is indispensable for evangelical political theology.

In an unpublished essay, Elia Nghikembua, late professor at Paulinum seminary, has vigorously supported the third alternative, in the belief that our understanding of the doctrine's abuse makes intelligible the theological conflict between the white and black churches, and that it provides a major resource for strengthening the church's political theology.[64] Nghikembua argues that far from the doctrine of the two kingdoms having been the cause of the traditional inability of the mission churches to assume an active political role, it is the recovery of the doctrine that can give their activism a solid theological base. Nghikembua points out that it was not until after the end of World War II that the doctrine of the two kingdoms began to be discussed in Namibia. Thus the doctrine itself cannot be said to be responsible for earlier passivity.

Nghikembua holds that the church is mandated to preach both law and Gospel, that is, its message is a dialectic of judgment and promise. God rules through both law and Gospel, or, to use Luther's vivid image, God's left and right hands, his wrath and his mercy, are servants of his love at work in his fallen creation. On the left, God's work of judgment and law includes the demand for justice. As such, it can be both a word of wrath and condemnation for the oppressor and a defense of the defenseless. On the right, God's work of unconditional love, his Gospel of promise, displays divine mercy and unmerited forgiveness, and is his eschatological gift of new life and salvation. In the classic two kingdoms tradition, the law of God is understood to have two major functions: the so-called spiritual use that exposes the human failure to achieve righteousness, and the so-called civil use that declares that society as a whole is obliged to obey the divine command for justice. It is not expected that the whole society be Christian (even during the days of late medieval Christendom), that is, that the society be in effect the church. The church, however, has as a part of its obligation, the task of proclaiming the divine command for justice, for all of society, to Christians and to non-Christians alike. God's law and its demand for justice thus provides the standard by which human culture is to be judged and transcends every culture's system of positive law.

In Southern Africa, however, he charges that the classic reformation doctrine has suffered profound distortion. While the Gospel, typically in a highly individualized form, was earnestly preached to both black and white, the law of God, specifically the so-called civil use understood as the divine demand for justice, was bypassed. Thus it was the lack of an authentic two kingdoms tradition that encouraged social passivity in both the German-language and African churches. Nghikembua argues that in Namibia the lack of a civil use of the law was disastrous. Instead of preaching the law of divine justice, the mission preached conformity to the law of the land, apartheid. Instead of the classic dialectic that holds the Word of God to contain both judgment on sin and mercy for the sinner, the mission's theology preached an obedience to the status quo coupled, however inconsistently, with the Gospel of life and salvation. Instead of a nuanced dialectic of law and Gospel, the mission settled for a convenient contradiction. Accordingly, the Gospel itself was undercut. Instead of being a word of unity for the faithful, the Gospel was not permitted to allow them to share in the fellowship of one church.

The issue is not purely academic. The church was tested publicly when the South African plan for the permanent imposition of apartheid on Namibia was announced in the Odendaal Plan of 1963. The churches at the time offered no protest because they believed they had no theological base from which to speak. Many asked: Was it not the churches' sole responsibility to preach the Gospel? Surely that did not obligate them to adopt a dangerous "critical attitude" toward the state. Increasingly, however, the African leadership and many of the younger missionaries found introducing the doctrine of the two kingdoms to justify the churches' noninvolvement in political affairs to be untenable. The argument that the church has no proper political responsibility could not salve the moral outrage engendered by the Odendaal Plan. Increasingly, a new argument began to be heard. Precisely on the basis of its obligation to bear witness both to God's rule of law and of grace, the church may not excuse itself from being an advocate of justice even if that implies a criticism of the government.

In Nghikembua's judgment, the 1971 Open Letter was theologically possible only because of the black churches' newfound confidence of its competence to "remind" the prime minister what God's law requires in the Namibian situation.[65] In fact, Nghikembua cites Martin Luther as an authority for the new political activism. "The primary function of the state is to serve its people. . . ."[66] If the government is forgetting and neglecting its important task, then," Nghikembua believes, "it is necessary to be reminded."[67] Nghikembua concludes that the church's protest against the South African government is based

[o]n Luther's solid doctrine of the two kingdoms. [The church] has done a tremendous job to remind the government of its *opus proprium,* that is to say, its proper work of justice and fairness among all the people in Namibia and South Africa. This is, of course, an *opus alienum* for the church. It is her left hand work, that is to say. . . . But if injustice and unfairness are prevailing in the secular kingdom, then the church stands under an obligation to take up her *opus alienum* because nobody is doing that work.[68]

The innovative feature of the Namibian reinterpretation of the two kingdoms doctrine is its central focus on ecclesiology. Rather than seeing the doctrine as a justification for the church's withdrawal from the theater of politics, Nghikembua's approach is the reverse. Equipped with a doctrine of the two kingdoms, the church is given both the freedom and the obligation to witness to divine demands for social justice. If God were only Savior and not Judge, if God only forgave sin and did not condemn it, perhaps the church could be expected to restrict itself to being a bearer of consolation. Nghikembua argues, however, that just as God in Christ has an *opus alienum,* an "alien work," so does the church. It is bidden to make public God's judgment on human evil, including political evil. In traditional Lutheranism that sort of witness has been in practice highly suspect since it implies a competence on the part of the church both to know the mind of God, and to be in touch with the salient political realities. In the land of the reformation the churches' unwillingness to bring the law of God to bear on the ideology of the Third Reich proved by its silence to imply approval. It is remarkable that in a land where the reformation churches cannot be said to have a very long history, they have found a theological authority, and a spirituality, that leads them in a quite new direction. The courage exemplified in Namibian Christianity has not, of course, been created by its theology, but is *its* Creator. Can the roots of that courage be discovered? And, if so, can they be made available to the church, and to the world at large?

Spirituality: Source and Promise

> I will praise you in our congregations
> For you have not despised your suffering ones . . .
> The day will break when all the ends of the earth
> Will behold and taste your righteousness.
> For the kingdom, the power, and the glory are yours forever.
> Even in this land. Amen
> —Ps. 22, paraphrase by Zephania Kameeta

Visitors to Namibia invariably comment on its exotic beauty. But far more arresting is the attitude of its people. Inheritors of a legacy of oppression by a succession of imperial powers, pawns in the current games of international politics, Namibians appear nonetheless to be preternaturally hopeful. It is clear to them that the superpowers have no intention of intervening as their liberators. The determination of their powerful neighbor to continue its occupation of their land remains unabated. Yet their certitude of their liberation remains firmly fixed. Since traditional African religion saw time as an endless cycle, bound by the rhythms of nature, the current Namibian sense of the future as the expectation of something new is particularly significant. The future is no mere continuation of the present. It bears the promise of a new day that will overcome the miseries of the nation's history. What are the sources of that confidence? What is its promise?

It would be a serious mistake to look to any single group as the nation's savior. No individual has emerged as the nation's liberator.

It is clear, however, that the churches have become the major advocates of their people's cause. And within the churches a strong chorus cries out for a new dispensation, a future of freedom. Zephania Kameeta, now serving as auxiliary bishop of the Evangelical Lutheran Church in South West Africa/Namibia (Rhenish Mission), has long been identified with the liberation movement within the church and activist political groups. As a member of the executive committee of SWAPO, Kameeta is closely associated with the major leaders in the nation's political liberation movement. His voice is particularly highly regarded within SWAPO itself. As an activist he is representative rather than unique. But it is just this representative character of Kameeta's witness that gives it its significance. While his theology is uncompromisingly liberationist, it does not rest on the Marxist analysis that has been widely influential in Latin American liberation theologies.[69] Contemporary European and American influences are freely acknowledged: Jürgen Moltmann, J. H. Oldham, Martin Luther King, and James Cone, in addition to South Africa's Beyers Naudé and Allan Boesak. But the real inspiriation for Kameeta's theology is not literary, but existential, personal, not academic. His total identification with the suffering of his people, coupled with an intimate knowledge of the Scriptures, are the prime source of his witness. Pietism's emphasis on the correlation of personal spiritual experience with the content of the Bible has yielded unanticipated consequences.

In a 1975 lecture in Afrikaans at the University of Cape Town, Kameeta identified himself as an advocate of black theology. That his theology has a modifier is itself no innovation, he argued.[70] After all, one can speak freely of European or American theology without creating a stir. The character of black theology is neither ethnic nor racial. It is not a syncretism comparable to that developed in the so-called Zionist or independent churches of Southern Africa. It is rather a theology informed by "the condition of wretchedness in which the oppressed live."[71] Not attempting a universal theology, Kameeta deliberately seeks to root his reflection on the meaning of revelation in terms of the social realities of contemporary Namibia. He asks: What does Christ have to do with this time, this place, as seen by those who are caught up in this "tremendous machinery of violence?" His theology, thus, is deliberately contextual. The intensity of that focus needs not lead to a narrowness of vision, however. Kameeta believes that the major themes of classical theology are enlivened by a Namibian contextualization.

Zephania Kameeta at a Katutura Rally. (*Courtesy of John Liebenberg/NCC.*)

GOD SPEAKS A LIBERATING WORD

Black theology does not begin with the oppressed, but with God. "God is essentially free . . . and in his freedom he created the world a free creation."[72] Specifically this means that the whole cosmos, Southern Africa as well as Europe, is destined to manifest the freedom of God. This God who longs and mourns for freedom does not address a vacuum, but a humanity in which hunger and poverty, racial discrimination and physical torture, are supported by a ruthlessly if legally enforced oppression. In this situation the good news of liberation is no abstraction, but a "word which was born in poverty on hard stone."

The prophetic tradition of the Old Testament, particularly the Book of Amos, has had a profound influence on Kameeta's theology. The popularity of a religion with no social conscience was the foil for Amos's castigation of Bethel. Its priest, Amaziah, was the champion of a cult that blessed a society that relentlessly oppressed its own people. Amos, his opponent, used "the vocabulary of God" to defy the religious establishment. Any religion, whatever its rhetoric, which serves to justify social injustice is an enemy of God. In our time, Kameeta charges that Southern Africa has become the equivalent of the Northern Kingdom of the eighth century B.C. Religion is applauded, now as then, but only because it has betrayed God's promise that the poor will receive justice. The Word of God for Kameeta is thus the articulation of God's judgment on the moral quality of human life in any time or place. It is the Word of God, then, which exposes South Africa's claim to represent "Christian civilization" as being self-serving propaganda designed to protect the regime from prophetic criticism. The Word of God and its prophetic servants cannot assume a posture of neutrality with respect to social injustice. "Neutrality has in fact no place in the vocabulary of God."[73] Church people, therefore, who seek to distance themselves from the agony that apartheid has generated, do so at the cost of substituting the word of a fallen world for the Word of God. The Pauline exhortation (Rom. 11:2) that the will of God is known not by conformation to the standards of the world, but by an inner transformation of those who serve him, underscores the impossibility of separating his word from a sacrificial dedication to his service.

CREATION IN THE IMAGE OF GOD

The biblical narrative of the creation of humankind in the image of God has frequently been obscured in traditional "white theology" by ignoring the basic element of the *imago Dei:* freedom.

The Creator who discloses his freedom by his creation of mankind wills it to be free.[74] For Kameeta, freedom is far more than the negative term it has become for those who use it to designate independence from restraints placed on the individual. Freedom is the positive gift that enables one to praise and serve God, a gift that enables human beings to withstand all oppression. To be created in the image of God is to be destined for freedom, which implies having the capacity to struggle against everything that would seek to rob one of one's God-given dignity. To speak of the image of God without identifying this dimension of one's identity will imply a failure to be committed to the struggle for freedom. Thus, to say yes to the ruling powers in today's Namibia is to say no to God's mandate; to say no to the oppressors is to affirm one's having been made in the image of God. "The image of God in which I have been created shows me the way in which I can live in this world as a free and authentic human being."[75] While freedom is every person's birthright, the actualization of freedom is possible for those who believe in the Word of God. This implies being opposed to every form of slavery, a refusal to close one's eyes to oppression in the world, a commitment to live in the world and for its liberation.

When a white speaks of a black in purely negative terms, for example, as a "non-white, . . . he destroys my God-given dignity," Kameeta argues. "And if I regard myself as a non-white, I stand outside the gospel; I commit a kind of suicide. When the white robs me of my God-given humanity, it is then easy for him to give me over to his gods," those social and political structures that guarantee his authoritative rule over all blacks.[76]

Being human is having one's eyes open to see what is wrong in society. It means being a champion for liberation in season and out. Being human means living in the Gospel, struggling for the Gospel in the world. One who treats another as inhuman becomes inhuman oneself, for a truly free person sees other persons as cohuman, and treats them accordingly. It is the obligation of the oppressed to lead the oppressor to acknowledge that the one oppressed is, in fact, a real human being.

SIN AND ITS CONSEQUENCES

Rejecting the pietist understanding of sin is a purely individual matter, Kameeta sees it as a sociopolitical fact. Specifically, sin is revealed "where people are oppressed and exploited, where people are governed by violence."[77] It follows that sin cannot be overcome merely by a subjective change in attitude. Sin can be exposed and destroyed only by the revolutionary word of liberation that comes from God, a word that addresses all of life.

The biblical basis for Kameeta's understanding of sin is given in Jeremiah 2:13. The heavens are appalled; the people of Yahweh have forsaken him and have chosen broken cisterns instead of his living waters. Sin is a turning from God in unbelief.[78] In the Bible to break with the Lord means to refuse to acknowledge his work on Israel's behalf; specifically it is a rejection of the central role of the exodus as his liberation of Israel. To forget the exodus, Yahweh's testament of freedom from slavery, is to reembrace slavery. To abandon the God of the exodus covenant for the sake of serving one's own interests is to fall into bondage again. When Israel trusts in the nothingness that is the final alternative to God, its whole life is one of sin. Since God rules the destiny of each person, the history of peoples, and the whole universe, to leave him is to live in sin. God has not broken his commitment to his people, however. Through his prophets he calls them back to their covenant of liberation. And in Jesus Christ he makes his decisive entry into human history as the Liberator of all peoples of the earth.

Like his prophetic namesake, Zephania Kameeta sees the sins of the community as a public defiance of God's righteousness. In our time sin shows itself as the deliberate denial that God through Christ has removed the walls of separation between himself and humankind, and the walls separating persons from each other.[79] The specificity of the biblical Zephaniah's castigation of Judah and her neighbors has been faithfully sustained. Kameeta charges:

> Southern Africa's racism which is proclaimed by laws and protected by a huge army, builds concrete walls of separation that leads to alienation, suspicion and hatred. The differences of nationalities, languages and cultures, which are gifts of grace to enrich and beautify humanity, are used by the apartheid regime as bricks to build the walls of separation between man and man. The true and visible sisterhood and brotherhood that has been based on the liberating Gospel of Jesus Christ is seen as the violation of the law and a threat to race, color and tradition. These three gods determine the whole way of life in South Africa and Namibia and are in the eyes of the State more important than the Holy Trinity. These three gods determine where I should feel at home, where I should relax or not, in which vehicle I should travel and which seat I should occupy in that vehicle, whom I should love, what kind of education I should receive and where I should get medical care, where I should worship and even where I should be buried. Whatever I think, speak or do, I am required to worship and glorify race, color and tradition.[80]

This extended passage clearly indicates that Kameeta understands his opposition to apartheid to be fundamentally religious. Southern Africa's absolutizing of race, color, and tradition as social values beyond the reach of criticism is scored as idolatrous. It is unmasked as a violation of the first commandment. The commitment that the established cult demands produces frightening consequences.

> The one who cares to oppose this "divine" system is banned or jailed and tortured, or deported or murdered. Those who benefit from this evil system because of their race and the color of their skins regard it as the greatest responsibility of their "Christian faith" to protect this *status quo*. They believe that their whole existence depends on that. In the South African and Namibian context you are a good person and a believer if you support this apartheid system. But when you oppose it, you become a danger for the society and the unbeliever.[81]

Thus, in spite of its highly visible public religion, Southern Africa is caught up in the consequences of its own idolatory. Drunkenness, divorce, theft, and murder are the result of the suffering that a sinful social situation has produced. Family life is systematically destroyed by the restriction of blacks to the so-called homelands and the related contract labor system that separates a husband from his wife and children for long periods of time. White racism with its institutional structures has generated deep hatred. But because black frustration cannot be directed toward its cause, blacks lash out and murder other blacks. Poverty leaves thievery in its train. But behind the evident misery in which the majority of the people are caught, lies a fundamental theological problem. The whites regard themselves as gods, their ideology as absolute. They cannot see the blacks as their neighbors. And the blacks fail to see that their only real lord is God, and they are made in his image. Black worship of the white is the source of black misery, a form of bondage that can only be overcome by the liberation that God gives.[82]

CHRIST THE LIBERATOR

The content of the Gospel is Jesus Christ. In Southern Africa, however, public policy has been so defined as to make "the white man and his ideology" the dominant factor in every situation. From that perspective Christ himself is "white," for example, one who blesses the status quo with his presence and thus effectively suppresses all who are black. Thus, once again in history the identity of Jesus Christ has become publicly controversial.

Kameeta's reading of the Gospels shows a Christ who, at every point, undercuts the assumptions of Southern Africa's "Christian civilization." The birth narratives of Christ disclose his solidarity with the poor and the oppressed. He was born, in Bethlehem, as one of them. The beginning of his public ministry, according to the baptism and temptation narratives, highlights his total identification with sinners. The kingdom he has come to herald is expressly for those in greatest need: the powerless, the poor, the dispossessed. His victory over temptation must be understood as his refusal to separate himself from the oppressed by using his extraordinary powers for his own aggrandizement. Thus, the temptation narratives explicate the point of the baptism: Jesus totally identifies himself with outcasts and sinners.

Jesus begins his mission with the word of the kingdom. "A new day has broken in; the bonds of oppression and unrighteousness are broken. Come to me and be my disciples as co-workers in the struggle for liberation. And so be my witness in this world."[83] Christ, the kingdom of God, has come into our midst. His coming is the announcement of freedom from oppression. His kingdom embraces all of life: the personal and the social, the economic and the political. Nothing is excluded as Jesus gives himself for the freeing of all from their bondage to unrighteousness and inhumanity.

The climax of the Gospels in the narratives of the passion and resurrection makes clear that the story of Jesus is not biography, but a demonstration of the good news that God is at work in the life, death, and final victory of his son. Through the resurrection Christ has broken the bonds of slavery and has given his people freedom. Thus, to continue to live as though death has conquered Christ, is to live in sin. As Christ has overcome the power of death, those who trust in him must proclaim his victory over slavery—even in Namibia.

It is clear that hope for Namibia does not arise out of its present situation. Only God's son, who became oppressed in order to free the oppressed and thus to show God's liberating power for the world, is Namibia's hope. In an age of revolutions, Jesus remains the greatest revolutionary of all. He calls the whites to reject their exploitative racism; he calls the blacks to believe in the freedom he brings. Only in Christ can a racially divided Namibia come together as one society, a nation based not on differences in language and color, but on the righteousness and love of God.[84] To preach Christ today requires a clear declaration that in him slavery has been nailed to the cross. The coming of Christ has given humanity a new future, a future of hope.

THE DISCIPLESHIP OF FREEDOM

The Gospel of Christ is both an announcement of God's liberation of humanity and a call to discipleship. The real enemies of the church are not the unbelievers who regard the church with disdain, but Christians who are afraid of the power of the rulers of the world. Because of fear Christians become false prophets. They devise theologies that make it possible for them to avoid ever having to confront the structures of unrighteousness. But the church knows of another legacy: Elijah, in obedience to the Lord, shook the foundations of Israel's faithless religion. John the Baptist was not afraid "to stand alone in the desert of injustice, hatred, and separateness."[85] This heritage of liberation continues into our own time. A Dietrich Bonhoeffer (a German Lutheran martyr who plotted Hitler's death) was prepared to "sacrifice my reputation and my honor" to give everything that he had for God's kingdom of justice and peace. Martin Luther King's refusal to put his own security before his vision of what is right showed that the disciple may be called to be the martyr. The parallel between the German church struggle and the Namibian situation has been particularly striking.

In Bonhoeffer's day, the overwhelming majority of the church leaders in Germany hoped that by making concessions they could buy the freedom of the churches from the pressure of the dictatorship. They thought that the private discussions of their problems with the dictator behind closed doors would guarantee their security. . . . It is frightening to see how this situation is repeating itself in Southern Africa with striking similarities.[86]

Kameeta sees South Africa's Beyers Naudé, Desmond Tutu, and Allan Boesak as living examples of churchmen today who, at great personal risk, place fidelity to God's kingdom above concern for personal security. The seriousness of discipleship in the Southern African context is tested in one's willingness to place loyalty to the kingdom of God above the claims of nation and race. For the disciple the message of Pentecost very clearly demonstrates the fundamental difference between apartheid and Christianity.

Apartheid by its very nature divides and destroys; Christianity unites and gives new life. Apartheid forces people of different tribes and cultures apart, creating hostility and enmity; Christianity announces

Jesus Christ as the life of the world and proclaims the good news of love to all, everywhere, to the end of time.[87]

What would commitment to this Gospel mean for Southern Africa? The first step would be the "sorrowful acknowledgement" by Christians that in their loyalty to racial, ethnic, and denominational ties they fail to manifest the reality of the church of Jesus Christ. Such repentance should not be reduced to mere feelings of regret. It needs have a public character, including a concerted resistance to all laws which deny the dignity and equality of human beings. Christians are weak. But they are also part of the body of Christ, who in his mercy, is able to do great things through them for the well being of all of his people.

The church's primary problem is not with those who are outside looking in, but with the bulk of its own membership that is only lukewarm in its loyalty to Christ. Defenders of apartheid within the church fail to see its incompatibility with the kingdom of Christ. Fear, prejudice, and idolatry characterize the moral life of the uncommitted.

> A fear of change which leads to a blind, fanatical obedience to the standards of the world and thus to spiritual suicide; a contempt towards those that have a different pigmentation of skin which thus leads to hostility and hatred; a worship of one's own race which implies a rejection of the dignity of other peoples.

The tragedy of Southern African Christianity lies in its unquestioning devotion to this demonic triad, a loyalty it claims to be consistent with belief in Jesus Christ. Religious leaders who champion the idology of apartheid are heralded as saints and heroes. Prayers are offered for strength and wisdom to assist them in the implementation of apartheid. Indeed, to do so is often described as an African Christian's greatest responsibility.

Authentic discipleship, simple obedience to the word of Christ, is quite another matter. Discipleship consists of recognizing the difference between the word of the cross and the word of the world: the word of the cross is folly to those who are perishing, but for us who are being saved it is the power of God. (I Cor. 1:18) The tension between the two is unmistakable.

> The Word of the cross calls people to reconciliation with God and with one another, while the words of this world mostly call people to enmity towards one another. The Word of the cross reaches us to bring redemption, while the words of this world want to rule and control. The Word of

the cross came to serve and give his life as a ransom for liberation, but the words of this world bring the weak and the poor into oppression so that the powerful can live still better. The words of this world enslave the people while the Word of the cross liberates people.[88]

It is true that every attempt one makes to live out the freedom given in Christ is perceived as an affront to the powers that be. Thus, free persons are painfully reminded each day that they are bound by institutionalized racism. A seventy-year-old elder must cheerfully address a fifteen-year-old lad as "master" or *"baas,"* while he, in return, is expected to respond, "Good morning, my boy." In a hundred ways, trivial and monstrous, they who have been made free in Christ are compelled to live as though freedom for them must ever remain an illusion, that human dignity can never be theirs.

In the Scriptures, freedom and suffering are not separate. A free person suffers because the way to redemption and liberation is painful and hard. In the prophets, and supremely in God's Son, the redemption that God bestows means confrontation with evil. Through the cross God reveals his glory; through the cross he redeems the oppressed. Freedom is not a status, nor a matter of linguistic competency or economic security. Freedom is being able to recognize the presence of evil in one's life and having the power to prevail against it. The freedom that Christ discloses is, above all, his identification with the oppressed. Freedom for those who are in Christ is the power to exercise that same solidarity. The common fallacy of the white liberals lies in just this: their attempt to substitute sympathetic talk for living identification with the oppressed actually works to keep the structures of oppression intact. If freedom is one's participation in the liberation of the oppressed, freedom is inseparably united with suffering. In this struggle the free person may be required to give up his status, family, possessions, perhaps even life itself. Freedom is not living by empty, random choices, determined only by egoism. It is participation in the struggle against all that degenerates one's sisters and brothers.

LIBERATION AND THE CHURCH

Kameeta vigorously rejects the charge of criticis who say he has abandoned the ministry of the Gospel for the sake of politics. While the word of the cross and the discipleship of suffering are central to the biblical witness, it does not follow that suffering, freedom, and the cross have nothing to do with the daily life of the Namibian people. Traditional ethnic loyalties are challenged by the word of the cross no less than the white's apartheid.

Let the fact that you are Nama, Damara, Herero, not be the most important. Only the fact that Christ died for you all should be important. Although you have different skin color, he has reconciled you through his blood. If you encounter each other you should ask, "Are you a Christian?" and not "Are you an Ovambo?" You have not been reconciled by money or military power or tribal affiliation but by the blood of Jesus Christ.[89]

The apparent ease with which European thinkers separate theology from political thought is not possible for Kameeta. Pastoral care for people in the congregations cannot ignore the social costs of apartheid. The preaching of the biblical message cannot bypass the prophetic insistence on national righteousness nor the Pauline expectation that reconciliation be faithfully expressed in the church's own life. Actually every level of the church's witness is caught up in a system that violates her own integrity. Kameeta believes

[t]he struggle in our land has to do not only with the liberation of Namibia, it goes further and deeper than that. The presence of the South African government is not just a political question, but is a threat to the gospel of Jesus Christ. Thus I see it as the task of every Christian to see to the knocking down of this government. The South African government and its supporters proclaim . . . especially by what they do . . . a message diametrically opposed to the gospel. While God tells us in Jesus Christ he has broken down the wall of separation between himself and us, and between us and our fellow men, the South African government produces and builds the wall of separation which brings about alienation, mistrust, prejudice, fear, hatred, and enmity. Therefore I see the struggle in South Africa, and especially here in Namibia, not merely as a political struggle [but one], in which all Christians are called to participate. And if this should happen, an armed struggle can be avoided, because the word of the cross is enough for us to be able to tackle this task. . . . Or should God withdraw from the history of this world, hand it over to the devils, and restrict himself to temples and church buildings?[90]

There is an understanding of the church implied throughout Kameeta's theology that is of major importance. We have already noted his preference for plural pronouns when speaking of the Christian. Creation, enslavement, liberation, discipleship, all his themes concern the solidarity of persons who are reconciled to each other in Christ. They are the church, the community of the living Lord. The church is not a timeless, motionless abstraction, remote from world events. She is the visible company of those who bear witness to God's liberating action in Jesus Christ. She is the nation of the new exodus, on the way to meet her coming Lord.

> The way on which she walks does not lead through an invisible para-disiacal world where justice and truth and love reigns, but goes through this world where people despise, suppress, and exploit each other. . . . The church does not walk her way in silence or neutrality, but she sings with a clear voice the song of victory and liberation.[91]

Like Mary's song, "this hymn lifts up the oppressed, the poor, and the despised from the dust and brings down the proud and mighty from their thrones."[92] Her music is no phatic flood of empty sentiment, but a primary witness to the victory of Christ, a sign of revolutionary transformation in the midst of a fallen world. In Namibia the church, which is faithful to Christ, is a persecuted church. Her faithfulness to her Lord inevitably impels her to oppose a regime of so-called law and order that has been designed to destroy human dignity. She is an ecumenical church who has found that the persecution by the world, no less than the unitive word of the cross, has revealed to the people of God their fundamental oneness. And the gates of hell shall not prevail against her.

The rugged clarity of Kameeta's theology exhibits distinctive emphases: a holism that sees human culture as an integration of spiritual, social, and political components; a contextuality that hears the Word of God speaking the language of late twentieth-century Namibia; a churchliness that sees the Christian life as a solidarity of the faithful under the sign of the cross. It would appear that both the legacy of pietism and the more recent recovery of two kingdoms theology have been left behind. Clearly Kameeta's witness is no mere echo of what has become well established. Is his thought, however, better understood as a break with what has preceded it, or a sign of the fertility of that heritage? Before entering into a fuller consideration of these larger issues, a few preliminary observations may be in order.

Pietistic individualism is still very much alive in Namibia today: Kameeta's message is as much a challenge to those within the church as it is word of protest against the South African occupation. The roots of that message, however, are basically the same as those that have nurtured Namibian pietism: a fundamental emphasis on Scripture as the primary witness to the Word of God, an emphasis that is utterly convinced that the God of the Bible is even now speaking his Word to his people with an urgency and solemnity that incomparably surpasses all merely human opinions. It is the clarity of this spirituality that quite vitiates those critics who hold public life off limits to the theologian. And the fabric of that spirituality, whatever its content, is pure pietism. That God speaks through his Word now with an immediacy and an ultimacy that no one may gainsay is a conviction common both to the founders of the Rhenish mission and to its son Zephania Kameeta. An existentialist reading of Scripture need not, however, always be individualistic. The vitality of corporate ties in the African world makes the directness of God's address a social, rather than only a private, event.

Kameeta's relation to the revival of two kingdoms theology is less obvious. He uses neither the vocabulary nor the agenda familiar to two kingdoms practitioners. When he speaks of the Gospel, for example, it is from a Synoptic rather than from a Pauline base that he operates. Gospel, for Kameeta, is the message of the kingdom of God with its rich diversity of judgment and promise, command and liberation. The Pauline (and distinctively reformation) stress on a Gospel of mercy and grace alone that stands in sharp contrast to a law of judgment on unbelief and sin does not appear. What we have seen, rather, is that the reformer's message of law and Gospel has been restated in a vocabulary of unusual forcefulness. The content of the preaching of law and Gospel as understood by reformation theologians, has not been lost. The announcement of God's judgment on human sin, in both its public and private forms, is resolute. The controversial issue as to whether the law of God properly gives guidance to Christians has clearly been answered in the affirmative: Christians are bidden to reject both spiritual and political apartheid. Furthermore, the unity of Christians is not only a gift, but an obligation. Finally, the focus on the Gospel as God's merciful affirmation of sinners and outcasts in the life, death, and resurrection of his Son is central to Kameeta's work. Law and Gospel have not been confused. The quality of human obedience to God's commands is not the basis for his continuing acceptance of the believer. What may be more pertinent, Kameeta has also avoided an alternative trap: announcing a doctrine of grace that is so "pure" as to be morally sterile—a problem that Paul early identified, a problem that still infects the church. In sum, Kameeta has found it possible, in his version of liberation theology, to restate the theology of his heritage faithfully and, what may prove no less important, he has done so with a sweep, a freshness, a passionate integrity, that rings true.

Recently a selection of his devotional works has been published, making it possible for a much larger audience to become familiar with his witness.[93] Unfortunately, his finest literary work was not included, but has now become available. His paraphrase of Psalm 22, and an original Litany for Southern Africa, display a spirituality of extraordinary intensity and range.

Jesus' use of Psalm 22 as his own prayer at his crucifixion has troubled delicate spirits. Did he really believe that God had forsaken him? For that matter, had God? What is one to make of the exultant conclusion to a prayer begun in such despair? Actually, as Kameeta shows, the psalm's power and truth lie precisely in its blunt juxtaposition of radical frankness and sublime faith. That is exactly the sort of contrast that captures the dynamics of Kameeta's own spirituality. The combination of the horror of the cross with the certitude of God's victory is not an incoherent contradiction, but a disclosure of the range of biblical spirituality itself.

Psalm 22

My God, my God, why have you abandoned me?
In my own words, Lord, I call to you
        for you alone understand me and have real compassion for me.
You alone know what it means when one is oppressed and despised.

I am a laughing stock of the people
        whom all the authorities in the land are pleased to despise.
It disgusts them to see me in their side streets;
In their newspapers they intentionally write of me onesidedly;
In their news articles I am known only as
        a thief, a murderer, a robber, a sluggard.

With their pass laws they surround me;
With harsh restrictions they enclose me.
In their eyes I am nothing but a thing
        which one may shunt from place to place,
        a thing with which one can do anything.
Of my voice, my longing, my feelings,
        they have no interest.

Lord, my God, I call to you not only on Sunday
        and not at designated hours.
Both day and night my prayer is an unending cry of need.

My tongue cleaves to the roof of my mouth;
On you I wait; Hurry and save me!
In the burning sun, in front of the pass office,
I stand with my companions in misery the whole day.
We are sent from one office to another
          and on the way between them
I am arrested as a vagrant.
To you I cry for help; Hurry and free me!
In the homelands, in the sheet metal huts
          (which in their radio broadcasts and in their newspapers
          they call "friendly dwellings for the aged")
I sit, abandoned, and without means;
And my hope is far away.
I wait for you; Hurry and free me!

I suffocate in the dust of their offices;
In my whole life am I to do nothing
          other than to clean and wipe dust away?
In their eyes my witnesses are of no more worth
          than a newspaper soaked with rain.
Deep within the question torments me:
"What is the meaning of my life?"
I wait for you; Hurry and save me!

With my coat and my tattered bag
I stand at the train station
Put out into the rain and cold.
Before the little window at the ticket counter
I stand trembling.
"May I purchase a ticket now?"
I wait for you; Hurry and free me!

But in all this I do not hear them speak of you!
I will praise you in our congregations
          for you have not despised your suffering ones;
You do not turn yourself away in silence;
You reveal yourself as the Savior of all humankind.
The day will break when all the ends of the earth
          will behold and taste your righteousness.
For the kingdom, the power, and the glory are yours forever.
Even in this land. Amen.[94]

The ecclesiastical character of Namibian ethics already referred to finds a deeply moving expression in a liturgical prayer, a litany. Its blunt honesty captures the plight of a people who have been consistently abused for generations, a people whose national epic is a passion history. A crucified Jesus is confessed as liberator, a Lord whose *via dolorosa* now crosses the Namib desert. He is seen as the liberator who conquers by the power of forgiveness. Though slain by the demons of race and color, in his resurrection he promises to recreate a new people in justice and love.

Litany for Southern Africa

You Are My Hope

Are they the rays of the rising sun
which I now see, or is this a dream?
> R. *Jesus, our Liberator, we hope in you.*

Are you here destroying unrighteousness
so that righteousness can triumph?
> R. *Lord, our Liberator, we hope in you.*

Do you wish to call me out of my little corner
into which I have fled,
Call me to do some sacrificial deed?
> R. *Jesus, our Liberator, we hope in you.*

Will you free me from fear and unbelief?
Free me for valor and faith?
> R. *Lord, our Liberator, we hope in you.*

If you are now at work in my land—and in me,
Let your will be done.
At this moment, full of anxiety, many have become
displaced persons in their own land,
arrested,
cross examined, beaten, bound and banned,
imprisoned, or killed
because they have broken "laws" and "regulations"
which daily shackle and humiliate them.
> R. *Jesus, our Liberator, we hope in you.*

I pray you Lord, for my brothers and sisters,
whom the security police have abused in shameful ways.
I pray that the truth of your son and his righteousness
will redeem us from all unrighteousness.
> R. *Lord, our Liberator, we hope in you.*

This is not only a struggle in our land,
it is a struggle for humanity, for the whole creation.
This is an ominous struggle against you,
the almighty Creator of heaven and earth.
> R. *Jesus, our Liberator, we hope in you.*

The wages are so small
it is impossible to buy enough food, clothing and shelter.
It is better to be satisfied with little,

than to have clothing and shelter with an empty stomach.
    R. *Lord, our Liberator, we hope in you.*
Have mercy, O Lord, on those who are manipulated by the
press, radio and film.
Have mercy on those who seek their refuge in the beer halls.
    R. *Jesus, our Liberator, we hope in you.*
Have mercy on the children who are indoctrinated in the schools,
and on their teachers who, consciously or unconsciously,
have given themselves over to this task.
    R. *Lord, our Liberator, we hope in you.*
Have mercy, O Lord, on those who are led astray by
blood money and empty promises.
As you spoke to Bartemaeus, speak with them so that they soon will
    be able to see.
    R. *Jesus, our Liberator, we hope in you.*
Unite us under the banner of freedom,
Hinder all who in word and deed proclaim the message of
separation and division.
    R. *Lord, our Liberator, we hope in you.*
Open the eyes of those who have established this system
of separation and oppression and of those who support it.
    R. *Jesus, our Liberator, we hope in you.*
And when the hour of freedom comes, even before it has
been grasped,
then let your endless, liberating love be revealed to
us in forgiveness.
    R. *Jesus, our Liberator, we hope in you.*
Let the day break when all, regardless of their race,
language and color,
will join hands and sing in harmony the song of
liberation, love and righteousness.
    R. *Lord Jesus, we hope in you: hear our prayer.*[95]

In recent years Kameeta has increasingly focused his attention
on the twin themes of ecclesiology and ethics.[96] As an auxiliary
bishop utterly committed to the liberation of his people, he clearly
finds these concerns highly compatible. His theology is no weighing
of scholastic argument and counterargument. It is a confession. It is
above all an act of trust in God, specifically an exploration of what
it means to confess Christ in a situation of massive oppression. It is
a discovery of the presence of the cross and resurrection with their
promise of new life in today's Africa. It is a concrete answer to the
question: "What difference does faith make?"

In traditional theology, ecclesiology has usually been treated as a
subsection in dogmatics or systematics while ethics, in the recent
past, has become a discipline in its own right. Kameeta's close

joining of ecclesiology and ethics, now also being proposed by
some American ethicists, springs from a specifically African context: both rise from an understanding of what it means to participate in the life of Christ crucified, Christ risen, for an oppressed
people. Ecclesiology thus is not seen as a exercise in polity. It is not
an apologetic for a denominational tradition. Ecclesiology is the
community's participation in the life of Christ today.

For Kameeta, that community is best understood as an extended
family, a community where all are brothers and sisters and where
none is master over the others. The fundamental characteristic of a
family, in his view, is its capacity to share. The members of a true
family share in the needs and joys of all. It is a broken family—a
sick church—whose members do not share common burdens and
hopes. Sharing, as a mark of the church, is not only embodied
centrally in Christ. It is grounded in the biblical vision of creation.

> Our interrelatedness as members of the Church of our Lord Jesus
> Christ and as participants at this time in the history of our one world is
> already given in the first lines of our Bible: In the beginning God created
> the heavens and the earth. (Gen. 1:1). I do not find in these first lines of
> the creation event the creation of the First, the Second, and the Third
> World! The only thing I see is the creation of the heavens and earth in
> God's one world. There is only one creation in unity and harmony.[97]

Family life does not imply uniformity. It should see itself as a
reflection of the Garden of Eden that is a place of great diversity. "If
you plant only white flowers in a garden, it does not look so
beautiful. God's garden, God's paradise, has many trees, many
flowers and streams, all with different shapes, different smells,
tastes and colors. And that is exactly the beauty of it."[98]

In the biblical narrative God's primordial design has been frac-
tured by sin, by rebellion. God's one creation is frustrated by
human divisions powerfully expressed in racism, hatred, greed,
violence, and death. To claim to confess Christ while passively
accepting these demonstrations of the power of sin as normal is to
deny the good news of Jesus Christ. These divisions defy God, the
Trinity.

> Confessing Christ while holding to a belief in the First, the Second, and
> the Third World is a denial of the unity of one world—and also of the
> unity of the one church. It is a denial also of the high priestly prayer of
> the Lord Jesus Christ in John 17:21 in which he says, "I pray that they
> may be one, Father; may they be one in us just as you are in me and I in
> you. May they be one so that the world will believe that you sent me."[99]

Hence the confession: we are God's one church in God's one creation. It is by participation in God's unitive work that the barriers of separation can be overcome. Such sharing can involve suffering, as Namibians well know. But in Christ suffering can also be seen to be vicarious and intercessory. "The tears cried in South Africa and Namibia are tears of all of us all over the world, tears of all creation."[100] Vigorously rejecting any of the newly popular sectarian views of the church, Kameeta repeatedly insists that the interrelatedness expressed in sharing does not stop at the church's boundaries. Commitment to the community of sharing implies commitment to all of humanity. To be quite specific, "[T]he people here in the United States of America cannot be quiescent while there is turmoil in Namibia. And we in Namibia cannot be quiescent when we hear of Star Wars because we know that is going to affect us."[101] True ecumenism is as inclusive as creation: the more interrelated humanity is, the more interrelated is the church of Christ.

The biblical source of the church's identity as a community of sharing is displayed in Christ. The meaning of Bethlehem is that Christ chose to live among human beings as a human being—thus sharing a totally human life. Note, however, that "God's incarnation did not stop at Bethlehem. The incarnation event is continued by Christians when they become as Christ their Lord: he who as a human being lived among other human beings."[102] It is faith in the incarnation of God that enables persons of faith to dare to be human in a world that is frequently cold and inhuman. Thus incarnation, too, means sharing. The biblical imperatives: love one another warmly as brothers and sisters, show respect for one another, share your possessions, be happy with those who are happy, and weep with those who weep, all spring from Christ's own total involvement in the lives of those with whom he lived. Thus,

> the church of Jesus Christ is a community of life. And the members of this community share their lives with one another and that which God gives every day in our world. Therefore, in fact, we are no longer strangers, we are one people in God's one world.[103]

Sharing is also the key to sacramental theology, and again the whole creation is involved. "When we participate in the Eucharist, our belonging together and sharing in life is radiated into the world. It confesses the oneness of all humanity. That is what the Eucharist means: the sharing of the bread and the cup. This is a sharing of that which God gave us, a sharing that is an act of forgiveness."[104]

Mission too is sharing. Christ's great commission, the command to go to all the people of the world with the Gospel, is much more than a move beyond national boundaries. It is an imperative to "go into one another's lives" for the church's mission is an expression of its very nature: to go into the world in mission is to share the love of God.

> By doing this we focus the eyes of this inhuman world in which we live on Jesus Christ. By sharing ourselves with one another and the things God gave us, we focus the eyes of the world on him who gave himself— his body and blood for all. By doing this we become truly human; we share in the act of incarnation. By doing this, by focusing the eyes of the world on Jesus Christ, we make a break with inhumanity. As truly human we enter a community of love and sharing. This is to proclaim the good news of liberation.

In actual fact, however, the church typically conforms to the economic barriers that divide human beings from one another.

> Without blinking an eye, Christians speak of rich and poor churches. This is a heretical description of the church which distorts the gospel and prevents true sharing. With this false understanding the church allows herself to be conformed to the standards of this world. This heretical phrase, "poor and rich churches," is not only used in those areas in God's one world where the church happens to be regarded as rich, but also in those parts of the world where the church is regarded as being poor.[105]

Thus economic differences are permitted to become more decisive than unity in Jesus Christ.

Kameeta's work in ethics is, if possible, even more pointed than his work in ecclesiology. His method is clear and coherent. He is not interested in an ethics of rules and duties. He spends no time calculating consequentialist probabilities. His focus rather is on relationships. It is in the theater of interpersonal relations that social values come alive. The stage is wide: its protagonists are God and the world. It is in Christ and the church that the dynamics of the God/world relationship are brought into focus. Once more the move between the biblical world and today's world is seen as self-evident and mutually illuminating. And the centrality of sharing as the basic category for understanding the life and witness of the church is developed further.

In ethics, as in ecclesiology, the foundation is Christology. As the incarnate Lord, Jesus is portrayed in the New Testament as the Son who left his Father's throne to become a servant. The rich became poor that he might make them rich. Poverty and service become the focuses for disclosing the moral life.

In the New Testament Christ is described as the one who, though rich, became poor for our sake. When the Magi came from the East, rich in this world's goods, they reverenced him who was "wrapped in strips of cloth" in a poor manger, perceiving him as being in fact richer than themselves. Even in his embrace of poverty, he proved far richer than they.

In his presence the rich of this world became poor and the poor rich. In his eyes the wealth of this world is nothing. It is poor and miserable. Those who believe in him not only in their souls (as we are told in some quarters) but with their whole being are the truly rich. Even in their material poverty and hunger they are rich. They are making many rich by confronting the structures of injustice, oppression and exploitation. What is it to be rich? It is to tell with deeds that Christ is Lord. It is to tell the lords of this world that the world and all that is in it belong to the Lord God, the creator of heaven and earth. Everybody must get an equal share of its resources and wealth. Nobody may oppress and exploit the other because God created all of us equally in his image and gave his world to us to share and live equally in its beauty and wealth.[106]

The first step in God's mission to make many rich is for believers to go out with empty hands to meet their neighbors for

[w]hen we go empty handed to one another, we can embrace. We can be filled with good things. But when we are loaded down with luggage, it is difficult even to shake hands. Thus when we meet empty handed, our possessions do not get in the way and . . . we can then be filled with God's rich gifts.[107]

Kameeta points out in this connection that one of the Namibian languages closely parallels the Hebrew in that the word for "peace," *shalom,* is the same as the word for "meeting." To meet someone is to make peace with her. To meet another person properly is to share peace with him. From this Namibian/Hebrew perspective, an interpersonal relationship is grounded in a concern for mutual well-being. Kameeta's whole ethic can be seen as a series of variations on the primacy of sharing for a moral life that seeks to become genuinely human.

In a country as rich as Namibia, but in which the majority of the population is reduced to grinding poverty, the plight of the poor is never out of sight and is theologically critical. Justice in this view is not a matter of the well off sending assistance to persons in need.

Nor is it a matter of merely sharing one's belongings. Sharing is participation in the struggle for justice. It is a concrete overcoming of the divisions of race, class, and wealth that pit persons against each other. In Southern Africa, unfortunately, the have-nots are regarded as mentally unsound, uncivilized, stupid, and as nonpersons. You are only regarded as a human being if you have thousands or millions (!) in your bank account.

Decisions made in greed are forced on the poor; exploitation and oppression are their daily bread. This divisiveness is not simply a matter of economics. It shatters the body of Christ. "It is painful to experience these things in the life and work of the church of Jesus Christ in this world."

Neutrality in the face of blatant injustice is a further block to sharing. Attempts in the West to justify a posture of neutrality in the conflict between the persistent Namibian emphasis on the imperative to implement Resolution 435 calling for the liberation of the country from South African rule versus South Africa's entrenched "structures of injustice, racism, and exploitation" is a flat betrayal of Christian fellowship. Neutrality has become a way to dodge the simplest claims of justice.

Kameeta fully supports the conventional criticism of the international economic order voiced by ecumenical bodies, Catholic and Protestant. The charge: the contemporary social-political system gives primacy to considerations of power and profit at the expense of justice, equity and solidarity for the people of the world. In today's world the churches have typically become captive to the economic *status quo*.

> When it comes to everyday realities, the materially weak sister or brother is expected to act according to the dictates of the [established political] order and to forget her or his structures, her needs and principles—which mostly are regarded as inferior or even non-existent. Sharing in this oppressive order can never be a blessing to anybody. It becomes a burden to the fellowship, a curse to the community of saints.[108] It suffocates the true fellowship and creates dependency, distrust and alienation among sisters and brothers. This "dominating sharing" is not a real sharing. It is a burden. It divides humanity and will ultimately destroy it.[109]

The fundamental weakness of the present world system is that it encourages domination on the one hand and dependence on the other. This pattern, typically assumed to be normal or natural, is a repudiation of the will of God set forth in Jesus Christ. It is not often recognized that the churches in the so-called Third World face a moral problem when they become dependent on the economic wealth that is derived from the dominance and power of the major industrial nations. Kameeta questions whether it is morally justifiable for Third World churches to accept assistance from Western churches that profit from an unjust economic order. Is it not true that the wealth of the churches of the industrial societies has been purchased at the expense of those who suffer in the poverty of the poor nations?

Once when traveling in West Germany Kameeta reports being asked to speak of the suffering of the Namibian people. He, of course, has often done so. But on this one occasion he countered with a request of his own. "Please, before telling you of Namibia, I would like to hear from you something of the plight of the 'guest workers' here in Germany. Namibia, after all, has no monopoly on social suffering. Is Western Europe quite without its own exploitation in the case of its foreign workers?" He continued, "[B]efore knowing what is going on in Southern Africa, it is imperative for Christians to know what is going on in their own area. This means that the church must take concrete action against injustice. It must cease to be part of the ongoing exploitation of the oppressed where it is." Speaking to a church assembly in Washington, D.C., Kameeta pointed out:

> [Y]ou cannot understand the situation of suffering people in Southern Africa if you do not understand the situation of the poor, the blacks, and the oppressed here in the United States. . . . There can never be a true sharing among the sisters and brothers in the one church of Jesus Christ while some of us are sharing in the complicity of the oppressive power structures of our societies while we are blind to the poor, the oppressed, in our midst.[110]

An ethics of participation rules out theft. Major international corporations, however, have been engaging in a concentrated theft of Namibia's resources for eighteen years. Decree number one of the United Nations Council for Namibia holds that

> [n]obody is entitled to search for, prospect for, explore, take, extract, mine, process, refine, use, sell, export or distribute any natural resources, whether animal or mineral, situated within the territorial limits of Namibia without the consent and permission of the United Nations Council of Namibia.[111]

The refusal of the multinational corporations to comply with this rule has seriously depleted the natural wealth of Namibia, thus guaranteeing that its own people will see none of it. Lacking a capacity to enforce its ruling, the U.N. Council for Namibia can only observe foreign exploitation of the country as legally permissible robbery from the poor. The theft of Namibian resources violates simple justice. It also contradicts the Word of God. "The earth is the Lord's." (Ps. 24)

Clearly, sharing means interdependence. In the fellowship of interdependence we enter one another's lives. This entry is an exercise in mutuality. What is typically seen in Namibia, however, is a one-sided entry into the life of others, an act of aggression. This is the psychological climate that apartheid has generated. Kameeta points out:

> White farmers in Namibia frequently claim, "I am doing so much for the blacks to work for me." What they do not realize is that their claim to be experts about our needs is in fact an act of arrogance. We do not want things to be done for us. We want to do things together with other people in the world. We do not want to be fed. We want to share. South African propaganda boasts of what the government is doing for black people in Southern Africa and what they are prepared to do for the rest of Africa through their formidable economic power. What is overlooked is quite simple. Black people do not want to have things done for us. We want to share in the doing.[112]

The world's fear of sharing springs from its fear of Jesus Christ. For Christ is the revelation of sharing both for God and for all humanity in God's one world.

Both ethics and ecclesiology are determined by a participation in Christ's suffering. Suffering, however, is a medium, not an end in itself. For

> [i]n our pain and in our fight against injustice, we are enabled to discover the value and beauty of life. We discover the meaning of unity and our interrelationships with all of humanity. In our suffering we discover the Son of Man sitting at the right hand of his Father, the glory of God.[113]

Namibia does not present the only modern instance of the apprehension of glory in the midst of struggle. Kameeta frequently recalls that

> [a] few hours before he was assassinated Martin Luther King said, "I have been to the mountain top, and I have seen the promised land. I have seen the glory of God."[114]

It is this vision of God's victory that makes the oppressed strong. It is this that makes the struggle possible. Namibians are not desperate; they are not overwhelmed. The beauty of the land stands as a testament of the goodness of God. The unity of the church, in spite of all divisions, is a gift of God. In the eyes of the powerful, Namibians are terribly weak, of no significance. But for those who seek God's power disclosed in the cross, "[o]ur weakness is God's liberating power which scatters the proud with all their claims. It brings down the mighty from their thrones and lifts up the lowly. It fills the hungry with good things. It sends the rich away empty."[115] Kameeta cites the faith of a young Namibian woman as a testimony that speaks for the whole community.

I believe that God's favor will shine upon our country like the morning sun, and our wounds will be quickly healed. He will always be with us in our struggle for justice and peace. His presence will protect us on every side amidst imprisonment, torture and death. And when we call upon him, he will answer and liberate us.[116]

What then is Kameeta's achievement? He brings his listeners to a holistic spirituality that resists the polarizations typical of the contemporary scene. As an auxiliary bishop of his church, he also serves as SWAPO's resident theologian, thus disabusing critics inclined to dismiss the church as politically irrelevant or SWAPO as a Marxist front. There is as wide a range of political views among SWAPO's members as there is of theological views among the membership of the church. Those diversities are no embarrassment; they are necessary rather if the struggle for freedom and integrity is to be authentic. Those who believe a liberation movement can spring from the Gospel will have no difficulty recognizing the coherence of Kameeta's vision. While apolitical theologians and nonreligious social critics can reject Kameeta's holism, in doing so they face a more formidable task: how to show how a biblical people can disassociate the Gospel presupposed in a Christian social ethic from the realities of social history.

A further demonstration of Kameeta's holism lies in his effective mix of African and global concerns, present and past. The traditional African affirmation of the interrelatedness of all of life takes on new credibility when played out on an international stage where the knowledge of history is prized. Racism in Southern Africa is related to racism in the United States—and Australia. Military terrorism in today's Namibia is of a piece with the colonialist oppression of the German period. And all of it is a moral outrage for all of it defies the clear biblical teaching that all persons are made in the image of God, that all are destined to be free.

Kameeta's most enduring legacy: he has shown that the tears of Namibia, today and in the past, and the promise for Namibia's tomorrow as discerned in the biblical message of salvation are not contradictories. They are as inseparable as the Gospel's conjunction of death and resurrection, of judgment and hope. Apart from such a specifically theological interpretation of the Namibian story, it would be easy, perhaps necessary, to conclude that a people who have suffered so heavily and for so long probably cannot anticipate a future substantially different. The biblical doctrine that it is to the lost that salvation is promised provides the basis for belief in an utterly different future.

And it is Kameeta's achievement to serve as the most articulate bearer of that promise. He does so not as a spinner of a unique tale, told and known by no one else. He does so as the representative of his people proclaiming a message that is as fully derived from them as it is addressed to them. In Africa the wise are characteristically seen as advocates, as mediators, rather than as originators of wisdom. The Gospel, whose provenance was the Middle East, is a message of mediation between God and humanity, between peoples of diverse cultures. It is Kameeta's achievement to be an advocate for his people, his church, his Lord—and to do so with the fire of a prophet of Israel and (another antinomy) with the humility of a good shepherd.

Symbiosis

The pietism of the missionaries found fertile soil in Namibia. Even when the most critical assessment of their efforts has been made, the lasting achievement of their work cannot be gainsaid. A profound Christianization of the Namibian people has occurred through the work of the missions and their converts. The attempt of Germany's commercial interests to establish a political empire in Africa has long since come to naught. But the simple faith of German and Finnish missionaries has penetrated deeply into the Namibian soul and shows every sign of enduring.

Pietism's emphasis on the personal appropriation of the message of Scripture for the transformation of the moral life was a liberating and creative gift. Missionary preaching enabled the Namibians to discover a whole new dimension of life: the dignity and eternal significance of the individual human being. Partially because of the remarkable numerical success of their evangelistic efforts, the discovery of the significance of the individual did not prove socially alienating as has been the case elsewhere. In a remarkably short time, whole tribes became Christianized. Thus the difficulty that Western individualism has had in attaching significance to the life of the community has not arisen in the Namibian churches. Individual worth and communal solidarity have not been seen as contradictories, but as mutually supportive. Evangelical disclosure of the paramountcy of the personal has not been purchased at the cost of suppressing the basic importance of social existence. In particular, the biblical emphases of Rhenish and Finnish pietism have flowered in a Namibian setting. Scripture is not viewed as a collection of ancient texts but as the message of God announcing his will for all who will hear: salvation, moral transformation, righteousness, and justice are recognized as deep biblical themes which address all of life. The moral earnestness that has characterized pietism generally can be reduced to a preoccupation with the trivial. It is the Namibian achievement to have avoided that trap. In its Namibian form pietism has found its way to address a host of cultural evils with an imperious and convincing insistence that, in God's name, they be stopped.

A second factor at work in the maturation of the Namibian churches has been their appropriation of the theology of the Reformation. Admittedly they have done this in concert with their sister South African churches. But the far more vigorous leadership offered by the Namibian churches in the anti-apartheid struggle provides a more realistic opportunity for testing the pertinence of classic theology for today's world. The reinterpretation of the Reformation utilized by the Namibians is not a local innovation. Theological conferences in Namibia and South Africa, drawing upon the resources of the international theological community provided by the Lutheran World Federation, have made the findings of twentieth-century scholarship available to the Namibian churches as well as providing them with critically important intellectual and moral support. This development is not without its own ironies, chief of which lies in the indigenous churches' ability to find a once obscured, but now reaffirmed, doctrine of the two kingdoms as a major theological ally in their struggle for political freedom. Europeans and Americans had hardly suspected that that would be possible. Puritanism has, on occasion, proved supportive of the democratic experiment. But the record of Lutheran pietism is less reassuring. Theologians from Ernst Troeltsch to Karl Barth have not hesitated to charge Luther himself with prime responsibility for a tradition of political passivity that, in effect, removes the state from churchly critique. The Namibians have not found it possible to agree. For them the message of the Reformation centers in the word of God understood as a dialectic of justification and judgment, of the demand for justice and the gift of righteousness, of law and gospel. The tendency of pietism to elide justice, law, and social judgment was the innovation. Luther's criticism of the church had been more vigorous than his critique of the state, in part because it was more richly deserved at that time and, in part, because it mattered more. While the Namibian recovery of the message of judgment as applicable to the political arena may seem to be a novelty, it is direct response to an obvious need. At the theological level the new political activism is based on the belief that Luther's own example offers the soundest hermeneutic for understanding his exuberantly paradoxical language. The Namibians have found less difficulty than many dualistically inclined Europeans in believing with the Catechisms that good government and physical health no less than forgiveness and eternal life are gracious gifts of a loving God.

A further element in the Namibian critique of its legacy from pietism lies in its vigorous ecclesiology. For the Namibians, as for the Reformation, the church is seen as the enclusive community of the people of God rather than as a hierarchial or bureaucratic institution. The divisive character of the Christianity introduced into Namibia in the nineteenth and early twentieth centuries, separates whites from blacks, and denomination from denomination. From the beginning, Lutherans, among others, were divided among themselves. The new affirmation of the unity of the church both as a gift of the Spirit, and as a challenge to overcome separations among Christians is central to the Namibian vision. Since the division of Christians along racial lines parallels and, in fact, anticipates institutional apartheid, Christian unity is seen as a moral as well as an ecclesiological imperative. Particularly striking is the maturity of ecumenical commitment among Anglicans, Lutherans, and Roman Catholics. The dramatic support given the black Lutheran churches by the then white leadership of the other two churches on the occasion of the publication of the Open Letter of 1971 marked a new day in ecumenical solidarity as well as for political activism. It remains to be seen whether significant theological dialogue among these churches will now occur.

From a cultural perspective the most difficult form of unity to achieve is that which crosses the color barrier. Such a move publicly demonstrates the church's opposition to apartheid within its own life. Anglicans and Roman Catholics have consistently maintained interracial ecclesiastical structures, while the Lutherans, Reformed, and Methodists have separate denominations for whites and blacks. An increasing willingness of the small white church to join with its sister black churches in publicly opposing the new, so-called interim government for Namibia installed by South Africa represents a remarkable shift in conviction, a notable instance of a church's capacity to overcome its own history.

Theologically, the most surprising element in the social vision of the Namibian churches lies in their rapid assimilation of classical Western democratic theory. This had not been a part of the doctrine of the missions. Nor has it been encouraged by imperial Germany or colonialist South Africa. Is it realistic to expect political democracy to emerge as an independent Namibia? A part of the answer may lie in the witness of the churches.

The responsibility of the League of Nations, and subsequently, the United Nations, for the administration of Namibia, has been a painful bone of contention since the end of World War I. Politically it has seemed that the nation's only hope for independence lay in the willingness of the international community to free it from South African rule. The early advocacy of the Namibian cause at the United Nations by the Anglican priest, Michael Scott, at the request of the Herero people, illustrates both the involvement of the churches in the liberation struggle and the belief that the United Nations has a fundamental responsibility to see Namibia achieve independence. It can be argued that Namibia's appeal to the United Nations has been simply politically expedient. However, the explicit and detailed use of the United Nations' Universal Declaration of Human Rights by the churches in their 1971 Open Letter indicates their theological affirmation of what is formally not a theological text. The substance of the churches' argument has already been considered. The theological rationale that lay behind that act of appropriation bears examination.

If the theology of the Namibian churches is derived solely from sixteenth- and seventeenth-century sources, it may be difficult to see how they can embrace human rights language inspired by enlightenment rationalism. Each of the thirty articles of the Universal Declaration is violated daily in Namibia. The violations occur not because of a failure of citizens to obey the law, but rather because Namibian law requires behavior that defies the principles enunciated in the articles. On the positive side of the matter, each of the six headings in the preamble affirms values that are basic to contemporary Christian social doctrine: all members of the human family have inherent dignity, and equal and inalienable rights that are the foundation of freedom, justice, and peace. The declaration does not, however, indicate the source of these rights. Neither natural law nor the moral traditions of the human family are cited. The ideological diversity of the contemporary world probably makes such explication impossible. This philosophical arbitrariness of the Declaration presents a challenge to its member states. Thus the 1971 Open Letter of the Namibian churches is an affirmation of their ability to recognize in such a document as the Universal Declaration a specific profile of the character of a just and democratic society. Theologically this capacity to enter the arena of political judgment is no problem for two kingdom ethicists. The kingdom on the left is founded on a belief in the actual presence of rationality and justice in all human communities and that implies the God-given competence of governments to rule responsibly and the capacity of human beings to live together in the furtherance of the common good. The ability of the Namibian churches to use classical theology as a metaethical base for grounding the doctrine of the Declaration in the religious tradition of their country is rich in implications for other societies. The Declaration is given roots that it is prevented from claiming for itself. Namibian ethics affirms a universal grounding for human dignity in a time when most moralities have had to settle for some form of cultural relativism that inevitably erodes the credibility of any transcultural moral claims.

The most provocative element in the Namibian ethical vision is that which has emerged from Africa itself. The tendency in European thought, and its theology, is to encourage distinctions to harden into separations. That a human being is both soul and body has been affirmed in both Africa and Europe for centuries. For the European, a problem immediately arises: How are these two separate factors to be related? Atheism's denial of the reality of the soul is in part an attempted solution to the intolerable irrationality created by the notion of the existence of parallel entities that never meet. For the African, soul and body do not need to be united for they have never been separated. They are, in fact, but different aspects of the one integrated person. To deny either spiritual life or bodily life is unthinkable. Both are necessary for sustaining vital relationships with the seen and unseen world. The African sense of the holistic character of human life has been well indicated by Desmond Tutu.

The African would understand perfectly well what the Old Testament meant when it said "man belongs to the bundle of life," that he is not a solitary individual. He is linked backwards to the ancestors whom he reveres and forward with all the generations yet to be born. He believes in what H. Wheeler Robinson called "corporate personality." Even today when you ask an African how he is, you usually in fact speak in the plural "How are you?" and we will usually answer, "We are well, we are here," or the opposite; he will not be well because his grandmother is unwell, his vitality will be diminished in so far as one member of the family has reduced life force.[117]

The congruence between African and Semitic mentalities has frequently been observed.[118] The polarities imported into Africa under pietist, enlightenment, and idealist labels have been given a respectful hearing and then immediately translated into the categories of traditional holism. Personal morality and social ethics flow in a common channel. Christ is the head of the whole church as well as the forgiver of hidden sin. And he liberates his people from all forms of bondage: the spiritual as well as the political. It is this pervasive and quite spontaneous sense of the reality of relationships, this confidence in the solidarities of life, that transforms the European legacy. Two consequences can be noted.

From an academic standpoint, there is little that is new in the Namibian witness. And yet it is all new. Here biblical pietism, Reformation theology, and enlightenment polity do not fall into the incoherence common in European history, but rest on a much older tradition which welcomes them all. No propositional system has been designed that contains these elements in all their diversity. Their own narratives assume, however, much of what African religion makes explicit: life, to sustain meaning, requires both freedom and human solidarity. Isolation is actual death. Community is the source and nurturer of life, both personal and public.

The second consequence has already been discussed in some detail. And it is the final test of the authenticity of the Namibian witness. How is it that the Namibian churches can be leaders in the struggle for political liberation and yet be faithful to a religious heritage often marked by political disengagement? Can one preach a theology of the cross and, at the same time, be a freedom fighter? How can these alternatives and the dualisms they represent be overcome? Do not these antitheses lead to paralysis? Or, perhaps require the suppression of a partial truth for the sake of an equally limited imperative?

John F. Taylor's description of the African world view as a vision of "cosmic oneness" has its concrete expression in the solidarity of family, tribe, and nation.[119] H. J. Bravinck has captured this cultural perspective well. "For the Europeans it is a maximum happiness to govern the world. The African thinks: nature is a fellow creature."[120] There is no doubt that the struggle for the future of Namibia is a contest as to who shall rule. The Namibian churches, however, are unwilling to permit that contest to be decided by those who will not acknowledge all citizens of the land as fellow creatures. In the long run the Namibian struggle is not a matter of who has the greater number of guns or is willing to mount the higher level of violence. What is finally at stake is whether an ideology of separation or a belief in the mutuality of all creation will be freely expressed. The commitment of the churches to the latter alternative is a measure of their faithfulness to the kingdom of God and their distance from a fallen world. What finally is most significant in these churches' witness is their capacity to overcome apartheid spiritually as well as politically. In Africa, if not elsewhere, evangelical piety and political democracy have met, not in combat or mutual indifference, but in symbiosis.

Appendix:
Appeal to Lutheran Christians in Southern Africa Concerning the Unity and the Witness of Lutheran Churches and Their Members in Southern Africa

The Basis of Unity

The Federation of Evangelical Lutheran Churches in Southern Africa (FELCSA) has been formed in 1966 with the aim to manifest the spiritual unity of the Evangelical Lutheran Churches in witness and cooperative action. They have stated their unity in acknowledging Holy Scripture as the norm of all church doctrine and practice. At the same time they have recognised the three Ecumenical Creeds and the Confessions of the Lutheran Reformation as a true exposition of the Word of God.

The Danger to the Unity of the Lutheran Churches and Their Witness

The confessional basis of the Lutheran churches obliges every Lutheran Christian, the individual church bodies as well as FELCSA to withstand unanimously alien principles which threaten to undermine their faith and to destroy their unity in the doctrine, in their witness and in their practice.

A number of clear statements on the faith, the unity and the witness of the Lutheran Churches in Southern Africa have been worked out in the past few years. In spite of these statements on our faith and its relevance to our witness in the situation of Southern Africa, alien principles are the following:—

1. An emphasis on the loyalty to the ethnic group which induces Lutheran Christians to worship in a Lutheran church depen-

dent on birth or race or ethnic affinities which insist that the Lutheran churches in Southern Africa remain divided into separate churches according to ethnic principles;

2. The belief that the unity of the Church is only a spiritual unity which need not be manifested;

3. The belief that the structures of society and the political and economic system of our country are to be shaped according to natural laws only, inherent in creation or merely according to considerations of practical expediency, without being exposed to the criterion of God's love as revealed in the biblical message.

As a result of the impact of these alien principles on our church life it has been possible to implement fellowship of the pulpit and of the altar between the Lutheran churches only to a very limited extent. It has not been possible to arrive at a church structure which bears witness effectively to our unity and which serves united action. In many cases our churches have not been in a position to take a clear stand on behalf of people whose freedom and whose rights are being curtailed and whose dignity is being hurt by the political, social and economic structures and by the legislation of the Republic of South Africa.

We confess our own participation in the sin and failure of our church to live out what has been given to her through Christ's redemption. In the Lord's Supper we encounter the crucified and risen Lord so that we may be received into his fellowship and be strengthened in the fellowship with one another.

We are also aware that those who accept racial divisions as guiding principles in the life and organisation of our churches and those who countenance the deprivation of human rights, dignity and worth of people, created in the image of God, deprive themselves of the fellowship of Christian believers.

Our Commitment

We invite Lutheran Christians to join us by committing themselves to this appeal to reject these alien principles and to prevent them from determining our personal attitudes and the practice of our churches. By committing ourselves to this appeal we pledge to work for a true and credible expression of our unity in faith and witness.

In this context we refer to the following statements, formulated at various Lutheran church conferences, which to us are a true interpretation of the Word of God and of our Lutheran confession, related to the South African situation:—

1. JUSTIFICATION BY GRACE AND ITS CONSEQUENCES FOR THE FULL MUTUAL ACCEPTANCE OF ALL MEN IN THE CHURCH AND IN SOCIETY

We believe that "God's grace is open to all men without regard to their achievements, their social or racial status. Full mutual acceptance of all men should be our answer to God's grace, leading to full participation in society".

2. THE CHURCH

We believe "that the church as the body of Christ is always a supernatural and never a political entity. Entry into this body depends not on birth or race or natural affinities, but only on the calling of God accepted by men and confessed in faith and baptism".

3. THE MANIFESTATION OF THE UNITY OF THE CHURCH AND THE DIVERSITY OF NATIONS, RACES, CULTURES AND TRADITIONS

We believe "that the Church of Jesus Christ is one in him, and that it is a major task of the Church to show this unity visibly before the eyes of men. Differences of race, language, customs and tradition are given by God for the enrichment of the Church, and should never be allowed to become a cause of division". We are aware that in the Church "peoples from all nations, races, cultures and traditions are called and assembled to the one people of God, to which they all belong together in one and the same way. The Church is not a community of people with no differences, but a community of those who, in spite and precisely on account of their diversity and unacquaintedness, belong together under the gospel. Therefore the body of Christ is being divided where the doctrine is taught that the Church has to be structured according to peoples, races, cultures or traditions. Structuring the church according to its diversity is permissible only insofar as the confession of the unity of all believers is not being made incredible to the world".

4. THE RELEVANCE OF CHURCH STRUCTURES TO THE MANIFESTATION OF THE UNITY OF THE CHURCH AND TO ITS WITNESS

We believe that "belonging to the one church and membership in the congregation, also in its organisational and juridical aspects, is not a problem of secondary importance, but belongs to the essence of the Church. All Christians, irrespective of race, through the sacrament of baptism are members of the one Church. Through the proclamation of the gospel and the sacrament of the altar they have a share in and a claim on the fellowship of all believers. Therefore, however for racial reasons wants to separate or to keep separate Christians by ways of organisation of our Church law and whoever does not grant a Christian of a different race at all times a share in and a claim on the sacraments and proclamation of the gospel, excludes himself from the fellowship of all believers. Therefore the one who is not prepared to admit a preacher in his own congregation to the proclamation of the Word and the administration of the sacraments, because he is of a different race, destroys the evangelical ministerial office and the unity of the Church".

5. THE DIGNITY OF MAN

We believe "that the dignity of human personality is a gift of God, which cannot be conferred, and must not be infringed by any human political authority".

6. THE RESPONSIBILITY OF THE CHURCH FOR THE WORLD

We are aware that "the Church has to bridge the divisions among men and to take concrete steps on local, regional, and national levels to be one Church in God's one world. In this way we will be better able to participate in the ecumenical task of proclaiming the Kingdom of God in Church and society".

We are aware "that the Church is the conscience of the people and must also be the conscience of the authorities. This is the injunction which the Church received from its master Jesus Christ. We must perform the pastoral and the watchman's office . . . otherwise we become guilty before the Lord God".

7. IMPLICATIONS FOR THE POLITICAL SYSTEM OF THE REPUBLIC OF SOUTH AFRICA

To us the political system now prevailing in the RSA appears "to be based on a number of errors and misapprehensions. We are convinced that this whole system needs to be radically reconsidered and reappraised in the light of the biblical revelation and of the general experiences of mankind".

"We affirm that a political system can be accepted as valid only insofar as it does not obstruct the will and purpose of God. "We affirm that the political system in force in South Africa, with its discrimination against some sectors of the population, its acceptance of the break-up of many families, its concentration of power in the hands of one race only, and the limitations it imposes on freedom, cannot be reconciled with the gospel of the grace of God in Jesus Christ.

"We affirm that this system in many ways hinders the exercise of Christian fellowship.

"We affirm that it is the duty of all Christian citizens of South Africa to study this system carefully and to work out definite and practical proposals by which it can be changed".

8. RECONCILIATION AND PEACE

We affirm that it is the task of the Church to "preach the gospel of reconciliation and not of violence". Christians are peacemakers sent out into the storm in order to change, in a non-violent struggle, oppressive structures and conditions.

9. THE SOURCE OF OUR RENEWAL

We are aware that fellowship with Christ implies "that we accept one another unconditionally as he accepted us; that we practise the brotherhood of Christians and that we recognise in every human being the image of God which he has imprinted on him; that the righteousness he has given to us becomes the criterion of our personal and social relations".

Chronology

1000–2000	African migrations from the north join earlier inhabitants, the San, in settling Namibia.
1485	Portuguese navigator Diago Cao plants a stone cross some 112 miles north of Walvis Bay.
1805	The London Missionary Society begins work among the Nama in the south.
1842	The Rhenish Mission Society takes over the LMS program and extends the mission to include the Herero and Damara.
1863–70	The Herero "war of liberation" from Nama domination is waged.
1870	The Finnish Missionary Society begins work in northern Namibia emphasizing medical care as well as evangelism.
1878	Britain annexes Namibian port of Walvis Bay.
1883	Adolph Luederitz purchases Namibian coastal strip.
1884	A German Protectorate is established in Namibia.
1886	Germany and Portugal establish Namibia's northern border by dividing Ovamboland.
1890s	Tribal chiefs sign "treaties of protection" with the German Empire.
1893	Hendrik Witbooi, Nama leader, is defeated by imperial troops.
1903	The Bondelswart rebellion is overcome by imperial troops.
1904–7	In the German-Namibian War, over 77,850 Africans are killed. Survivors' cattle and land are taken by the Europeans.
1915	German authorities surrender Namibia to the Union of South Africa.
1919	"South West Africa" is entrusted to administration of South Africa as "a sacred trust of mankind" by the League of Nations.
1920–23	South Africa quells revolts of Ovambo, Nama, Rehoboth groups. In 1922 one hundred are killed.

1920s	Increasing numbers of Germans and Afrikaners settle in Namibia.
1925	A Contract labor system is formally established, requiring all Africans to carry permits when outside assigned areas.
1930s	South Africa proceeds to incorporate Namibia as its fifth province.
1946	South Africa refuses to recognize the United Nations' claim to exercise the League of Nations' responsibility for Namibia.
1946	A third of the membership of the Rhenish mission leave to join the African Methodist Episcopal Church in protest over the mission's support of South African policies.
1949	Michael Scott represents Chief Hosea Kutaku in petitioning the United Nations to replace South Africa as trustee for Namibia.
1957	The Ovambo People's Organization (OPO) formed and reorganized in 1960 as the South West Africa People's Organization (SWAPO) as a multiracial national liberation movement in spite of the government's refusal to recognize nonracial political organizations.
1960	Leonard Auala is named the first African to head a Namibian church, the Evangelical Lutheran Church in Namibia (ELOC).
1964	South Africa's apartheid system is extended to Namibia by the Odendaal Commission Report: Africans to be restricted henceforth to their appointed rural areas.
1966	The U.N. General Assembly terminates South Africa's mandate and claims direct responsibility for administering Namibia. SWAPO begins armed struggle against South African rule.
1967	The U.N. Council for South West Africa determines independence to be achieved by June 1968. Thirty-seven SWAPO leaders are tried under South African security laws. Andimba Toivo Ya Toivo, SWAPO's co-founder, is arrested and sent to South Africa's Robbin Island prison.
1969	The U.N. Security Council terminates South Africa's mandate over Namibia.
1971	The International Court of Justice declares South Africa's occupation of Namibia to be illegal. Church

leaders issue an Open Letter calling South Africa to abide by the ICJ ruling. Some 15,000 workers stage a two-month strike in protest over the contract labor system.

1972   Anglican bishop Colin Winter and staff are exiled from Namibia.

1973   The U.N. General Assembly recognizes SWAPO as "the authentic representative of the Namibian people." The church printing press in the north is bombed.

1974   The U.N. Council for Namibia requires its approval for the removal of any natural resources.

1975   Angola becomes free from Portugal. South Africa invades Angola, assisted by the United States. South Africa convenes the Turnhalle Conference in Windhoek to lay plans for an "independent" Namibia. SWAPO is excluded.

1976   The U.N. General Assembly grants SWAPO full observer status as Namibia's representative. The Security Council passes Resolution 385 calling for national elections under U.N. supervision

1977   South Africa transfers Namibia's port, Walvis Bay, to direct South African administration.

1977   The Western Contact Group (Canada, France, the United Kingdom, the United States, and West Germany) negotiates with South Africa to plan for an "internationally acceptable election" in Namibia.

1978   South Africa accepts the Contact Group's plan with qualifications. In May, South Africa attacks a refugee camp at Cassinga, Angola: 612 Namibians are killed. In July, SWAPO accepts the Contact Group plan; subsequently South Africa rejects it. In September, the U.N. Security Council passes Security Council Resolution 435, calling for the implementation of the Contact Group's plan. South Africa conducts the Turnhalle Conference elections in Namibia. The U.N. declares the elections to be illegal.

1979   South Africa places 80 percent of the population under martial law. It arrests all SWAPO leaders inside Namibia.

1980   Using Namibia as a staging area, South Africa invades Angola with 4,000 troops. It occupies the southern part of Angola. The rebuilt church press at Oniipa is bombed a second time.

1981   The Western Contact Group's Geneva conference on Namibia collapses after SWAPO agrees to all conditions but South Africa walks out. The Anglican seminary is bombed.

1982   The U.S. proposal to link implementation of SCR 435 to Cuba's withdrawal of its troops from Angola is condemned by the U.N. General Assembly.

1983   South Africa launches another major invasion of Angola via Namibia.

1984   Andimba Toivo Ya Toivo is released from prison. South Africa refuses new proposals for implementing SCR 435.

1985   Northern Namibia closed to all persons not having special authorization. South Africa installs puppet government in Windhoek.

1986   Headquarters of the ecumenical anti-apartheid agency, the Council of Churches in Namibia, is destroyed by fire. South Africa announces that it will allow SCR 435 to be implemented only when Cuban troops leave Angola. Angola refuses linkage, claiming the Cubans are necessary for Angolan defense against South African aggression.

Ai-Gams Declaration: Ecumenical (Anglican, Catholic, Lutheran, Methodist) and political (SWAPO plus nine other groups) consensus calling for all Namibians to reject South African rule and to seek immediate implementation of SCR 435.

1987   Some 100,000 South African troops are based in northern Namibia. Africans protest military terror; multiple atrocities against civilians are committed.

1988   Oshakati bank bombed; 17 killed. Churches hold South African agents responsible. South Africa agrees to return troops from Angola and to allow United Nations supervised elections in Namibia in 1989 if Cuban troops will have been withdrawn from Angola.

1992   Target date for the unification of 360,000-member Evangelical Lutheran Church in Namibia (ELCIN), 190,000 member Evangelical Lutheran Church in South West Africa/Namibia (ELC), and 12,000-member German Evangelical Lutheran Church (DELC).

Notes

Chapter 1. Tribes and Empires

1. Current population estimates vary somewhat. The U.N. Institute for Namibia concludes that the total population today includes 1,035,000 blacks, 115,000 coloreds, and 100,000 whites. The area is 824,269 square km (318,261 square miles). One of the tribal legends speculates that the violence of nature strikingly visible in the Namibian landscape, could only have been the work of a god capable of both anger and creativity.

2. Hans Jenny, *South West Africa, Land of Extremes* (Windhoek: South West African Scientific Society, 1976), p. 37.

3. Ibid, p. 41. Note the use of biblical and Afrikaans (South African Dutch) names—a sign of the gradual Christianization of the tribes.

4. Hendrik Witbooi, *The Diary of Hendrik Witbooi* (Cape Town: C. Voights, 1929).

5. Otto von Weber, *Geschichte des Schützgebietes Deutsch-Suedwest-Africa* [History of the German Southwest Africa Protectorate] (Windhoek: Verlag der S.W.A. Wissenschaftlichen Gesellschaft, 1979), p. 9.

6. J. Metzkes, *Otjimbingwe Aus Alten Taken Einer Rheinischen Missionsta-tion in Hererolande, Südwestafrika 1849–1890* [Otjimbingwe, an early Rhenish mission station in Hereroland, Southwest Africa 1849–1890] (Windhoek, 1962), p. 20, quoted in Jenny, *South West Africa,* p. 45.

7. Jon Manchip White, *The Land God Made in Anger* (Chicago: Rand McNally, 1969), p. 251.

8. In 1877 the British annexed the Walvis Bay area, but were reluctant to press further claims.

9. Quoted in J. L. de Vries, *Mission and Colonialism* (Johannesburg: Raven Press), p. 11.

10. The German Colonial Society had been able to reach an advantageous settlement with the imperial government. The society would gain rights for developing mineral deposits in the territory settled by the Rehoboth Basters, the Herero, and various Nama groups. African ethnic authorities were not excluded from the negotiations, but it is not likely that they understood the nature of the wealth they would lose—in exchange for protection from each other. In any case, they realized no financial profits from the transaction. Cf. de Vries, *Mission and Colonialism,* p. 10.

11. In 1889, it would become necessary for the German government to take over the management of the mines and place them under the direction of a commissioner supported by imperial military and administrative forces.

12. Quoted in de Vries, *Mission and Colonialism,* p. 21f.

13. Ibid, p. 23.

14. Ibid.

Notes

15. Cf. George M. Frederickson, *White Supremacy, A Comparative Study in American and South African History* (New York: Oxford University Press, 1981.)

16. Rohrbach's argument is summarized in de Vries, *Mission and Colonialism*, p. 41.

17. Quoted by Jon M. Bridgman, *The Revolt of the Hereros* (Berkeley: University of California Press, 1981), p. 51.

18. Horst Dreschler, *Südwestafrika Unter Deutscher Kolonialherrschaft* [South West Africa under German colonial rule] (Berlin, 1955), p. 349, quoted in Bridgman, *Revolt of the Hereros*, p. 62.

19. F. Fabri, *Die Entstehung Des Heidentums* [The origin of paganism], p. 4, quoted by de Vries, *Mission and Colonialism*, p. 97.

20. Quoted in de Vries, *Mission and Colonialism*, p. 146.

21. Bridgman, *Revolt of the Hereros*, p. 44.

22. From *The Diary of Hendrik Witbooi*, quoted in Bridgman, *Revolt of the Hereros*, p. 45.

23. Drescher, in his *Südwestafrika*, speaks of von Francois's policy as one of "annihilation."

24. Bridgman, *Revolt of the Hereros*, p. 148.

25. As a movement within German Lutheranism, pietism was initially a reaction against scholastic orthodox theology and the authoritarian cast of traditional church life in favor of a personal appropriation of the message of Scripture. This emphasis on religious experience typically issued in a stress on moral earnestness—sometimes leading to puritanism. Particularly in the nineteenth-century, pietism fostered initiatives in world evangelization, ministries of mercy for the sick and disabled, and the reestablishment of the female diaconate. In Africa, pietism's interpretation of religion as a social reality accessible to all proved particularly congenial. Witbooi's understanding of his own life experience as a parallel to the biblical saga reflected a favorite pietistic theme.

26. Bridgman, *Revolt of the Hereros*, p. 1.

27. Ibid.

28. Heinrich Loth, *Die Christliche Mission in Südwestafrika* [The Christian mission in South West Africa] quoted in Bridgman, ibid., p. 21.

29. C. H. L. Hahn, *Native Tribes of South West Africa*, in Bridgman, *Revolt of the Hereros*, p. 21.

30. Welling, *South West Africa*, p. 191, quoted in Bridgman, ibid., p. 90.

31. de Vries, *Mission and Colonialism*, p. 27, quoting from Pfeil, *Deutsch-Südwest-Afrika Jetzt Und Später* [German South West Africa now and later] (München: Lehmanns Verlag, 1905).

32. Ibid. The colonialists' understanding of the justice appropriate for an African colony was illustrated in the regulations issued by the *Deutsche Kolonialbund,* the settler's union in Windhoek: every colored (i.e., African) person must regard a white person as a superior being. In court the evidence of one white man can only be outweighted by the evidence of seven colored persons. (Cited by Peter Fraenkel, in *The Namibians of South West Africa,* quoted by Edward C. May, *Report on the Wingspread Conference in Namibia,* Racine: The Johnson Foundation, 1976, p. 6).

33. Bridgman, *Revolt of the Hereros*, p. 61, quoted from Theodor Leutwein, *Report on the Natives of Southwest Africa and Their Treatment by Germany* (London, 1918), p. 55.

34. Bridgman, *Revolt of the Hereros*, p. 111.

35. Ibid., p. 112.
36. Ibid., p. 125.
37. Ibid., p. 126.
38. Ibid.
39. Ibid., p. 127.
40. Ibid.
41. Ibid., p. 145.
42. Ibid., p. 164.

Chapter 2. Missions, Churches, and Politics

1. G. Parrinder, *African Traditional Religion* (New York: Harper, 1976), pp. 40ff.

2. Kwesi I. Dickson, *Theology in Africa* (Mary Knoll, N.Y.: Orbis, 1984), p. 52f.

3. Seppo Löytty, *The Ovambo Sermon* (Tampere, Finland: Luther-Agricola Society, 1971), p. 116.

4. C. Wandres, *Über Das Recht Der Naman Und Bergdaman* [The system of law of the Nama and the Bergdamara], 1901, quoted by the Namibian theologian Johannes Lukas de Vries in *Mission and Colonialism in Namibia* (Johannesburg: Raven, 1978), pp. 33ff.

5. Any viable Namibian future will require a revival of justice and a recovery of law. A new nation will bring not an annihilation of an ancient moral sense, but its rebirth as the people's strongest defense against the incursion of alien cultures that rejected its claim to its own land.

6. Heinz Hunke, *Namibia, the Strength of the Powerless* (Rome: IDOC International, 1980), p. 80.

7. Excerpt from *Berichte der Rheinischen Missiongesellschaft* [Reports of the Rhenish Mission Society], 1885, quoted in Karl H. Hertz, *Two Kingdoms and One World* (Minneapolis: Augsburg, 1976), p. 96.

8. Ibid.

9. Ibid.

10. Pastor Paul, "Die Mission als Erzieherin der Eingeborenen in unseren Kolonien," *Flugschriften der Hanseatischen-Oldenbugischen Missions-Conferenz* ["The mission of the teacher of the natives in our colonies," *Pamphlets of the Hanseatic-Oldenburg Mission Conference*] (Bremen: Hanseatischen-Oldenburgischen Missions-Conferenz, 1904), in *Nationalität und internationalität in der Mission,* [*Nationality and internationality in the mission*] quoted in Hertz, *Two Kingdoms.*

11. Ibid.

12. Ibid.

13. Julius Richter, "Besteht eine Gefahr der Verweltlichung unseren Missionslebens?" ["Will our missions survive the danger of secularization?"], quoted in Hertz, *Two Kingdoms,* p. 97.

14. Friedrich Fabri, *Die Stellung des Christen zur Politik* [The position of the Christian in relation to politics] (Barmen, 1863), in Hertz, *Two Kingdoms,* p. 98.

15. de Vries, *Mission and Colonialism,* p. 5.

16. Mary Fulbrook, *Piety and Politics, Religion and the Rise of Absolutisms in England, Wuertemberg and Prussia* (Cambridge: Cambridge University Press, 1983).

17. Ibid., p. 179.
18. Schoenberg, *Diary,* quoted by de Vries, *Mission and Colonialism,* p. 136.
19. de Vries, *Mission and Colonialism,* p. 81.
20. From this perspective, it is surprising that any individual missionaries, in spite of their background, ever did dare question the wedding of empire and mission. It is even more remarkable that the African people would trust the mission sufficiently to respond positively to its message since the missionaries were, in African eyes, identified with the imperial forces. Nonetheless, the unlikely happened. The Rhenish Society, and its sister, the Finnish Mission Society, against heartbreaking odds, proved to be astonishingly effective. Today over half of the nation's population are members of the two daughter churches of these missionary efforts. Another 30 percent of the population is Roman Catholic, Anglican, Dutch Reformed, and Methodist, giving us a nation which, statistically at least, is far more Christian than is the United States.
21. "Hirtenbrief der Rheinischen Mission an die Herero-Christen," *Rheinische Missionsberichte* ["Pastoral letter of the Rhenish Mission to the Christian Herero," Rhenish Mission reports], 1904, quoted in Hertz, *Two Kingdoms,* p. 100.
22. According to Hannah Arendt, a true revolution always involves a new beginning for a people and springs from a "new story" heard as having supreme importance for them. "The course of human history suddenly begins anew, an entirely new story, a story never known or told before, is about to unfold." Hannah Arendt, *On Revolution* (New York: Viking, 1963), p. 28.
23. For an analysis of the preaching in the Ovambokavango Church based on the models of Finnish pietism, see Löytty, *The Ovambo Sermon.*
24. It may be salient to note that while the Rhenish mission is Evangelisch, that is, a Protestant effort representing a Lutheranism moderated by important Reformed elements, the Finnish mission and its daughter church more clearly represents a pietist/orthodox Lutheranism.
25. Namibia is commonly referred to in the English literature by two other names: German South West Africa and South West Africa. The former refers to the territory during the time of the German protectorate, 1884–1915. In 1967 the United Nations recognized "Namibia" (derived from the time of the great Namib desert) to be the appropriate noncolonial name for the country.
26. Quoted in *Namibia in the 1980s* (London: Catholic Institute for International Relations and the British Council of Churches, 1981), p. 10.
27. The Nama had lost their grazing land to the Germans and were reduced to surviving by hunting wild animals with trained dogs. To force the Nama to seek work as laborers for white farmers, a heavy dog tax was imposed. It was their protest against this threat to their livelihood that evoked their brutal repression.
28. For a detailed, autobiographical account of the "Windhoek massacre," see John Ya-Otto, *Battlefront Namibia* (Westport, Conn.: Lawrence Hill & Co., 1981), chap. 3.
29. For a description of the plight of labor in Namibia, see chap. 7, "The African Condition," in Alfred T. Moleah, *Namibia, The Struggle for Liberation* (Wilmington, Del.: Disa Press, 1983).
30. Marion O. Callaghan, *Namibia: The Effects of Apartheid on Culture and Education* (Paris: UNESCO, 1977), p. 43.
31. Ibid.
32. It has been estimated that there are at least forty political parties in Namibia, most of which are small and are identified with specific ethnic constituencies. Such groups as the South West Africa National Union (SWANU) and the

SWAPO-Democrats, a SWAPO splinter group, have limited support. While SWAPO's membership is predominately black, it has white members, both German and English speaking, as well.

33. *Windhoek Observer,* (17 July 1982.

34. Ibid.

35. In older literature, Ya Toivo is frequently referred to by his European name, Herman Toivo ja Toivo.

36. Quoted in Colin Winter, *Namibia, the Story of a Bishop in Exile* (London: Lutterworth, 1977), p. 43.

37. "It was hell to have to shoot at women," reported a South African Defense Force spokesman in the *Johannesburg Sunday Times* of 7 May 1978, as quoted by Winter in *The Breaking Process* (London: SCM Press, 1981), p. 22.

38. Figures given by John Evenson, "The Day the Soldiers Came," *Namibia Newsletter,* Spring 1988, p. 1.

39. Henning Melber, *Our Namibia* (Atlantic Highlands, N.J.: Zed Books, 1986), p. 151.

Chapter 3. An African Vision

1. T. Dunbar Moodie, *The Rise of Afrikanerdom* (Berkeley: University of California Press, 1975).

2. Ibid, p. x.

3. Ibid, p. 1. This belief in national history, as being a history of salvation, is found elsewhere in the Christian world, specifically where the Calvinist tradition has been influential, most notably, of course, in the United States.

4. Ibid.

5. *Journal of Theology for Southern Africa* (Braamfontein: South African Council of Churches, June 1977, pp. 9, 12). Is the Calvinism of the Afrikaner churches, for all of its massive political influence, faithful to the theology of the Calvinist Reformation? For a negative answer, see Roy J. Enquist, "A Tillichian Analysis of Afrikanerdom," in *Being and Doing, Paul Tillich as Ethicist,* edited by John J. Carey (Macon, Ga.: Macon University Press, 1987).

6. Hertz, *Two Kingdoms,* p. 71.

7. Ibid, p. 87.

8. Ibid, p. 91.

9. Engle, in Ulrich Duchrow, *Lutheran Churches—Salt or Mirror of Society?* (Geneva: Lutheran World Federation, 1977), p. 132.

10. Ibid, p. 136.

11. This interpretation of the two kingdoms attempts to apply isolated Luther texts to twentieth-century politics, quite disregarding the development of Enlightenment democratic theory during the interim, which the Reformers could not have anticipated. Here is a vivid illustration of how a noncontextual reading of religious documents can generate highly dubious conclusions.

12. Current plans call for the relocation of Paulinum from its remote site at the old mission station, Otjimbingwe, to the capital, Windhoek.

13. Department of Information and Publicity, *SWAPO of Namibia, To Be Born a Nation,* (London: Zed Press, 1971), p. 167.

14. Ibid.

15. Hens Jenny, *South West Africa, Land of Extremes* (Windhoek: South West African Scientific Society, 1976), p. 201.

16. Gunnar Listerud, ed., *The Lutheran Teaching on the Two Kingdoms* (Umpumulo: Lutheran Theological College, 1967), p. 17.

17. Ibid, p. 27.

18. Ibid, p. 223.

19. Ibid, p. 224.

20. Ibid.

21, President Hahne, "Statement by the Church Leadership of the ELCSA-H" in Hertz, p. 250. For a detailed analysis of the response to the Umpumulo Memorandum, see Wolfram Kistener, "The Context of the Umpumulo Memorandum of 1967," in Ulrich Duchrow, *Lutheran Churches*, pp. 165ff.

22. Zephania Kameeta, *Why, O Lord?* (Philadelphia: Fortress, 1986), p. vii.

23. Ibid.

24. "Open Letter to His Honour the Prime Minister of South Africa" and "Letter to the Congregations," Church Boards of the Evangelical Lutheran Ovambokavango Church and the Evangelical Lutheran Church in South West Africa (Rhenish Mission), Windhoek, 1971.

25. Ibid.

26. *The Evangelical Lutheran Church in South West Africa (ELC)* (Windhoek: Evangelical Lutheran Church, n.d.), p. 8.

27. Ibid. For a discussion of varied Lutheran responses see Hertz, pp. 251-66. More significant, perhaps, was the ecumenical support the Open Letter quickly evoked. Colin O'Brien Winter, Anglican bishop of Namibia, released the following statement of support on 25 July 1971:

> Bishop Leonard Auala and Moderator Paulus Gowaseb have produced an important document. It behooves all people of this territory, and especially those who govern us from Pretoria to read it, but best of all to listen to what these men are saying. . . . [The Letter] confirms what all of us who have contact with the blacks know to be true, that the overwhelming majority of blacks in this land totally reject apartheid. The Bishop and the Moderator make five points why this is so. They are (1) that blacks are not free people in this land; (2) that free movement is denied them; (3) that blacks are afraid to express their opinions for fear of reprisals; (4) that voting rights are denied black peoples; (5) that job reservation hinders the development of black peoples and destroys their family life. . . .
>
> They expose apartheid as a violation of the Declaration of Human Rights upon which every free nation of the world bases it laws. New schools, new hospitals, new roads, new Bantustans all beg the real issue. The black man is still suffering in this land, is still exploited, is still denied those basic human rights without which life in the modern world becomes intolerable. These two Christian leaders are telling me loud and clear that they and their people are not free, that they yearn for freedom and that they can never be free in a state which bases its legislation on racial discrimination. . . . I agree with their assessment of the situation as it exists in South West Africa today, and I stand by them in their views. . . . Apartheid must be denounced as unacceptable before God. Who else but the leaders of the Churches can do this? (Colin Winter, *The Breaking Process*, pp. 165ff).

The two Roman Catholic bishops of Namibia published their strong support of the Lutheran Open Letter in the Namibian public press. The text is given in *The Green and the Dry Wood* (Windhoek: Oblates of Mary Immaculate, 1983), p. 10f.

28. The support given by the Anglican church in Namibia would prove to be especially vigorous. Its bishop, Winter, who was deported in 1972, was the chief architect of his church's Maseru Declaration of 1978; which protested the systematic persecution of the churches by the government. The very publication of the declaration was enough to serve as immediate cause for the deportation of Winter's successor, Vicar General Ed Morrow. For the text of the declaration, see Winter's *The Breaking Process* (London: SCM Press, 1981), pp. 46–48.

29. For a compelling, detailed autobiographical account of the nature of such torture, see John Ya-Otto, *Battlefront Namibia* (Westport, Conn.: Lawrence Hill & Company, 1981).

30. The government's hostility to the churches' activism is not difficult to understand. In June 1976 the Lutheran and Anglican bishops wrote to Henry Kissinger, U.S. secretary of state, who had announced that he would be meeting with Prime Minister Vorster, that as South Africa's policies "have destroyed human dignity and bedeviled relationships with the family and community, and totally alienated the black population," South Africa should be required to leave the country—exactly the position of SWAPO.

31. The member churches of the CCN, which represent about 80 percent of the Namibian population: the African Methodist Episcopal Church, the Anglican Diocese of Namibia, the Congregational Church, the Evangelical Lutheran Church in South West Africa/Namibia (ELOC), the Evangelical Reformed Church of South West Africa, the German Evangelical Lutheran Church, the Methodist Church, and the Roman Catholic Church.

32. "An Open Letter to the Prime Minister of the Republic of South Africa," Windhoek: Executive Committee of the Council of Churches in Namibia, February 1983.

33. Ibid.

34. Ibid.

35. "Open Letter to Christian Churches in Europe and North America," Windhoek: Executive Committee of the Council of Churches in Namibia, May 1984.

36. Ibid.

37. "A Statement of the Executive Committee," Windhoek: Council of Churches in Namibia, January 1985.

38. Ibid.

39. *The Green and the Dry Wood,* The Roman Catholic Church (Vicariate of Windhoek) and the Namibian Socio-Political Situation, 1971–1981 (Windhoek: Oblates of Mary Immaculate, 1983).

40. "Lutheranism has, as it were, given German paganism room to breathe. By teaching creation and Law from the Gospel, Lutheranism has accorded paganism something like a sacral sphere of its own. The German pagan can invoke the Lutheran doctrine of state authority as a Christian justification for National Socialism." Karl Barth, *Eine Schweizer Stimme, 1835–45* [A Swiss Voice, 1835–45]. (Zurich: Evangelischer Verlag, 1945), pp. 133ff.

41. K. Kirschnereit, "Open Letters," 1972–74, quoted in Hertz, *Two Kingdoms,* p. 259.

42. Hertz, *Two Kingdoms,* p. 258.

43. Ibid., p. 260.

44. Ibid.

45. Ibid.

46. Ibid., p. 261.

47. K. Kirschnereit, "Evangelism ohne Ideologie" ["Evangelism without ideology"], *Allgemeine Zeitung,* Windhoek, 12 July 1973, quoted in Hertz, ibid., p. 258.

48. Albertus Maasdorp, *In die Welt—für die Welt* [In the world—For the World] pp. 28ff., quoted in Hertz, ibid., p. 256.

49. The Swakopmund venue for this regular annual meeting of the Federation of Evangelical Lutheran Churches in Southern Africa served to underscore the

urgency of the Namibian situation. Delegates at Swakopmund represented the three Namibian churches: the Evangelical Lutheran Church in South West Africa, the Evangelical Lutheran Ovambokavango Church, and the German Evangelical Lutheran Church in South West Africa; the four large black South African regional churches that have since merged to form the Evangelical Lutheran Church in Southern Africa: the ELC, Cape/Orange Region, Southeastern Region, Transvaal Region and Tswana Region; in addition, three small German speaking South African churches: the Cape Church, the Hermannsburg Church, and the Transvaal Church; plus the Rhodesian and Moravian churches.

50. Federation of Evangelical Lutheran Churches in Southern Africa: Braamfontein, South Africa, 11–13 February 1975.

51. Ibid.

52. Ibid. For the full text of the appeal, see the Appendix.

53. Arne Sovik, ed., *In Christ—A New Community,* Proceedings of the Sixth Assembly of the Lutheran World Federation (Geneva: LWF, 1977), p. 180.

54. Ibid.

55. *Bonhoeffer: Exile and Martyr* (New York: Seabury Press, 1975).

56. Albred Burgsmüller and Rudolf Weth, *Die Barmer Theologische Erklärung* [The Barmer theological declaration] (Neukirchen-Vluyn: Neukirchener Verlag, 1984), p. 36.

57. Statement of Martin A. Sövik of the Lutheran Council of the United States of America before the Subcommittee on African Affairs, U.S. House of Representatives, 21 February 1985.

58. Heinz Hunke and Justin Ellis, *Torture—A Cancer in Our Society* (Windhoek: Oblates of Mary Immaculate, 1987).

59. The Lutherans were prepared to have the archbishop of Finland present to signal ecumenical support for Hurley.

60. Conversations with younger theologians suggest that in Namibia as elsewhere, this emphasis on reconciliation may not be able to be maintained indefinitely. There is no doubt that the present leadership of the churches unhesitatingly envisions the church as a community of reconciliation.

61. Oral comments by Bishop Dumeni to a U.S. church delegation in Namibia in 1985.

62. Ibid.

63. Ibid.

64. Elia Nghikembua, "The Two Kingdoms Doctrine in Namibia and South Africa," 1983. Professor Edward Schroeder of Christ Seminary, St. Louis, Missouri, has graciously shared this essay with the author. Critically injured in an automobile accident on a main road near the Paulinum seminary, Nghikembua was discovered by a white policeman who, because of the pastor's color, refused to take him to the hospital. By the time black help could be summoned to do so, Nghikembua had died. The policeman did manage to salvage Nghikembua's few possessions, but under apartheid, had been unwilling to come to the aid of their owner.

65. Ibid, p. 22.

66. Ibid. Martin Luther, *Luther's Works* (Philadelphia: Fortress, 1962), 45:80.

67. Ibid.

68. Ibid, p. 24.

69. Perhaps this is not surprising since Marxist literature is banned in both Namibia and South Africa. Kameeta's home at Otjimbingwe has been raided repeatedly by South African police in unsuccessful attempts to find banned

literature. Namibian theologians have been relatively freer to have access to American black theology and West European political theology.

70. "A Black Theology of Liberation," in Gerhard Tötemeyer, *South West Africa/Namibia* (Randburg: Focus Suid Publishers, 1977), pp. 225ff.

71. Ibid., p. 225.

72. Ibid, p. 226.

73. Ibid.

74. Theo Sundermeier, *Christus, Der Schwarze Befreier* [Christ, the black liberator], (Erlangen: Verlag der Evangelisch-Luthrischen Mission, 1973), p. 97.

75. Ibid.

76. Ibid, p. 96.

77. Tötemeyer, *South West Africa, Namibia* p. 227.

78. Sundermeier, p. 101.

79. Zephania Kameeta, "The Confessing Church in Southern Africa and Her Message of Justice, Liberation and Reconciliation," n.d. p. 8.

80. Ibid, p. 7f.

81. Ibid, p. 9.

82. Sundermeier, p. 105.

83. Ibid.

84. Ibid.

85. Kameeta, "The Confessing Church in Southern Africa," p. 12.

86. Ibid.

87. Ibid, p. 15.

88. Ibid, p. 16.

89. Kameeta, "The Word of the Cross," in *A Call to Prayer for the People of Namibia* (Geneva: Lutheran World Federation, 1983), p. 4.

90. Ibid, p. 5.

91. Tötemeyer, *South West Africa/Namibia* p. 221.

92. Kameeta, *Confessing Church*, p. 2.

93. Ibid.

94. Kameeta, *Why, O Lord?* Psalms and Sermons from Namibia (Philadelphia: Fortress, 1986).

95. German text in Sundermeier, *Christus, Der Scharze Befreier*, p. 46. My translation.

96. German text in Theo Sundermeier, *Zwischen Kultur and Politik* [Between culture and politics], (Hamburg: Lutherisches Verlagshaus, 1978), p. 106. My translation.

97. The following citations are from an unpublished address given by Kameeta at the first annual assembly of the Metropolitan Washington Synod, Evangelical Lutheran Church in America, 6 May 1988.

98. Ibid.

99. Ibid.

100. Ibid.

101. Ibid.

102. Ibid.

103. Ibid.

104. Ibid.

105. Ibid.

106. Ibid.

107. Ibid.

108. Ibid.

109. Kameeta frequently stresses, "We in Namibia confess every Sunday, the *communio sanctorum,* . . . our hope in the manifestation of the kingdom of justice and peace."

110. Metropolitan Washington Synod address.

111. Ibid.

112. Ibid.

113. Ibid.

114. Ibid.

115. Ibid.

116. Ibid.

117. Ibid.

118. Desmond M. B. Tutu, "Some African Insights and the Old Testament," in Hans-Jürgen Becken, *Relevant Theology for Africa* (Durban: Lutheran Publishing House, 1973), p. 44.

119. In addition to Becken, *Relevant Theology,* cf. Aylward Shorter, *African Culture and the Christian Church* (Maryknoll: Orbis Books, 1974).

120. John V. Taylor, *The Primal Vision* (London: Penguin, 1963), p. 72.

121. Löytty, *Ovambo Sermon,* p. 75.

Bibliography

Amsterdam, Alton Louis III. *Namibia Report* 14, no. 3. New York: U.S. World Journal, 1988.

Arendt, Hannah. *The Origins of Totalitarianism.* New York: Meridian Books, 1958.

Barth, Karl. *Eine Schweizer Stimme, 1835–45.* Zurich: Evangelischer Verlag, 1943.

Beetham, T. A., and Noel Salter, ed. *The Future of South Africa.* London: SCM Press, 1965.

Bethge, Eberhard. *Bonhoeffer: Exile and Martyr.* New York: Seabury Press, 1975.

Boesak, Allan Aubrey. *Farewell to Innocence: A Socio-Ethical Study on Black Theology and Power.* Maryknoll, N.Y.: Orbis Books, 1977.

Bridgman, Jon M. *The Revolt of the Hereros.* Berkeley: The University of California Press, 1981.

Burgsmüller, Albred, and Rudolf Weth. *Die Barmer Theologische Erklärung.* Neukirchen: Neukirchener Verlag, 1984.

Callaghan, Marion O. *Namibia: The Effects of Apartheid on Culture and Education.* Paris: UNESCO, 1977.

Cubitt, Gerald, and Johann Richter. *South West.* Cape Town: C. Struik (Pty) Ltd., 1967

Desert Conflicts. London: British Council of Churches and CIIR, 1981.

de Vries, J. L. *Mission and Colonialism.* Johannesburg: Raven Press, n.d.

Dickson, Kwesi. *Theology in Africa.* Maryknoll, N.Y.: Orbis Books, 1984.

Duchrow, Ulrich, ed. *The Identity of the Church and Its Service to the Whole Human Being.* Geneva: Lutheran World Federation, 1977.

———. *Two Kingdoms—The Use and Misuse of a Lutheran Theological Concept.* Geneva: Lutheran World Federation, 1977.

Eirola, Martti, et al. *The Cultural and Social Change in Ovamboland, 1870–1915.* Joensuu, Finland: University of Joensuu, 1983.

Elert, Werner. *The Structure of Lutheranism.* Saint Louis: Concordia, 1962.

Ellis, Justin. *Education, Repression & Liberation: Namibia.* London: Catholic Institute for International Relations, 1984.

Enquist, Roy J. "Afrikaner Religion as a Model of Liberation Theology," *Dialog.* Summer 1978.

———. "A Tillichian Analysis of Afrikanerdom." In *Being and Doing, Paul Tillich as Ethicist,* edited by John J. Carey. Macon, Ga.: Macon University Press, 1987.

———. "Fac Jesum Regnum," *Dialog.* Fall 1985.

Fredrickson, George M. *White Supremacy, A Comparative Study in American and South African History.* New York: Oxford University Press, 1981.

Fulbrook, Mary. *Piety and Politics, Religion and the Rise of Absolutism in England, Wuertemberg and Prussia.* Cambridge: Cambridge University Press, 1983.

Grosc, LaVern K., ed. *Sent Into the World.* Proceedings of the Lutheran World Federation Fifth Assembly. Minneapolis: Augsburg, 1971.

Hertz, Karl H. *Two Kingdoms and One World.* Minneapolis: Augsburg, 1976.

Hunke, Heinz. *Namibia, the Strength of the Powerless.* Rome: IDOC International, 1980.

―――― and Ellis, Justin. *Torture—A Cancer in Our Society.* Windhoek: Oblates and Mary Immaculate, 1978.

Jenny, Hans. *South West Africa, Land of Extremes.* Windhoek: South West African Scientific Society, 1976.

Johanson, Brian, ed. *Human Rights in South Africa.* Johannesburg: South African Council of Churches, 1974.

――――, ed. *The Church in South Africa—Today and Tomorrow.* Johannesburg: South African Council of Churches, 1975.

Journal of Theology for Southern Africa. Braamfontein: South African Council of Churches, June, 1977.

Kairos Theologians. The Kairos Document, Challenge to the Church. Grand Rapids, Mich.: Eerdmans, 1986.

Kameeta, Zephania. "The Confessing Church in Southern Africa and Her Message of Justice, Liberation and Reconciliation," n.d.

――――. "The Word of the Cross." In *A Call to Prayer for the People of Namibia.* Geneva: Lutheran World Federation, 1983.

――――. *Why, O Lord?* Geneva: World Council of Churches, 1986.

Laukkanen, Jukka R. *Reflections Upon the Early Finnish Mission Work in Namibia in Light of Christian Freedom.* M.A.R. thesis, Lutheran Theological Seminary Library, Gettysburg, 1988.

Listerud, Gunnar, ed. *The Lutheran Teaching on the Two Kingdoms.* Umpumulo, South Africa: Lutheran Theological College, 1967.

Löytty, Seppo. *The Ovambo Sermon.* Tampere, Finland: Luther-Agricola Society, 1971.

Luther, Martin. *Luther's Works,* vol. 45. Philadelphia: Fortress, 1962.

Mau, Carl H., Jr., ed. *In Christ—Hope for the World.* Proceedings of the Lutheran World Federation Seventh Assembly. Geneva: Lutheran World Federation, 1984.

May, Edward C. *Report on the Wingspread Conference on Namibia.* Racine: The Johnson Foundation, 1976.

Melber, Henning. *Our Namibia.* Atlantic Highlands, N.J.: Zed Books, 1986.

Moleah, Alfred T. *Namibia, the Struggle for Liberation.* Wilmington, Del.: Disa Press, 1983.

Moodie, T. Dunbar. *The Rise of Afrikanerdom: Power, Apartheid, and the Afrikaner Civil Religion.* Berkeley: University of California Press, 1975.

Motlhabi, Mokgethi, ed. *Essays on Black Theology.* Johannesburg: University Christian Movement, 1972.

Namibia. Philadelphia: American Friends Service Committee, 1981.

Namibia in the 1980s. London: Catholic Institute for International Relations and the British Council of Churches, 1981.

Nghikembua, Elia. "The Two Kingdoms Doctrine in Namibia and South Africa." Christ Seminary-Seminex, St. Louis, 1983.

Okullu, J. Henry. "Church-State Relations: The African Situation," in *Church and State,* Opening a New Ecumenical Discussion. Geneva: World Council of Churches, 1978.

Parrinder, G. *African Traditional Religion.* New York: Harper & Row, 1976.

Schoeman, Stanley, and Elna Schoeman. *Namibia* (World Bibliographical Series). Oxford, Santa Barbara, Denver: Clio Press, 1984.

Shorter, Aylward. *African Culture and the Christian Church.* Maryknoll: Orbis Books, 1974.

Soggot, David. *Namibia, the Violent Heritage.* London: Rex Collings, 1986.

Sovik, Arne. *In Christ—A New Community.* Proceedings of the Lutheran World Federation Sixth Assembly. Geneva: Lutheran World Federation, 1977.

Sundermeier, Theo. *Christus, Der Schwarze Befreier.* Erlangen: Verlag der Evangelisch-Lutherischen Mission, 1973.

————. *Zwischen Kultur und Politik.* Hamburg: Lutherisches Verlagshaus, 1978.

————, ed. *Church and Nationalism in South Africa.* Johannesburg: Raven Press, 1975.

SWAPO of Namibia. *Report on Torture and Atrocities Committed by Racist South Africa in Namibia Since January 1987.* New York: SWAPO of Namibia, 14 July 1987.

————, Department of Information and Publicity. *To Be Born a Nation.* London: Zed Press, 1981.

Taylor, John V. *The Primal Vision.* London: Penguin Books, 1963.

The Evangelical Lutheran Church in South West Africa (ELC). Windhoek: Evangelical Lutheran Church, n.d.

The Green and the Dry Wood. The Roman Catholic Church and the Namibian Socio-Political Situation, 1971–1981. Windhoek: Oblates of Mary Immaculate, 1983.

This Is Namibia, A Pictorial Introduction. London: International Defence & Aid Fund, 1984.

Tillich, Paul. *The Protestant Era.* Chicago: University of Chicago Press, 1948.

Tötemeyer, Gerhard. *South West Africa/Namibia.* Randburg: Focus Suid Publishers, 1977.

Tutu, Desmond M. B. "Some African Insights and the Old Testament." In *Relevant Theology for Africa,* edited by Hans-Jurgen Becken. Durban: Lutheran Publishing House, 1973.

United Nations. *Plunder of Namibian Uranium.* New York: United Nations, 1982.

United Nations Council for Namibia. *The Military Situation in and Relating to Namibia.* New York: United Nations, 1984.

————. *A Summary of Twenty Years of Effort by the Council for Namibia on Behalf of Namibian Independence.* New York: United Nations, 1987.

United Nations Department of Public Information. *Objective: Justice* XV, no. 1, June 1983.

U. S. Foreign Policy and South Africa's Illegal Occupation of Namibia. Washington, D.C.: Washington Office on Africa, Africa Subcommittee of the Foreign Affairs Committee of the House of Representatives, Congressional Ad Hoc Monitoring Group on Southern Africa, Congressional Black Caucus, 1987.

von Weber, Otto. *Geschichte des Schutzgebietes Deutsch-Suedwest-Afrika.* Windhoek: Verlag der S.W.A. Wissenschaftlichen Gesellschaft, 1982.

Wee, Paul A., ed. *The Church and the Namibian Quest for Independence.* Geneva: Lutheran World Federation, 1987.

White, Jon Manchip. *The Land God Made in Anger.* Chicago: Rand McNally & Co., 1969.

Wilson, Francis. *Migrant Labour in South Africa.* Johannesburg: South African Council of Churches and SPRO-CAS, 1972.

Winter, Colin. *Namibia, The Story of a Bishop in Exile.* Grand Rapids, Mich. Eerdmans, 1977.

————. *The Breaking Process.* London: SCM Press, 1981.

Witbooi, Hendrik. *The Diary of Hendrik Witbooi.* Cape Town: C. Voights, 1929.

Working Under South African Occupation: Labour in Namibia. London: International Defence & Aid Fund, 1987.

Ya-Otto, John. *Battlefront Namibia.* Westport, Conn.: Lawrence Hill & Co., 1981.

Index

African chiefs: Jonker Afrikaner, 20; Wilhelm Christina, 27; Jacobus Isaak, 27; Samuel Isaak, 44; Shikongo Kalulu, 23; Kamaherero, 31; Hosea Kutako, 63, 86; Frederich Maharero, 63, 86; Samuel Maharero, 20; Manasse, 27; Mweshipandeka Shaningika, 23; Nicodemus, 29; David Witbooi (son of Hendrik), 86; Hendrik Witbooi (son of Moses), 21, 27, 31, 32, 34, 35, 38, 44; Kupido Witbooi (grandfather of Hendrik), 21; Moses Witbooi (father of Hendrik), 21; Samuel Hendrik Witbooi, 63

African culture, 60

African Methodist Episcopal Church, 85

African people, 77

African peoples: Damara, 20; Herero, 20; Kavango, 20; Nama, 20, 21; Ovambo, 20, 23, 27; Rehoboth Basters, 20; San, 20; Tswana, 20. *See also* separate entries

African religion, 10, 45, 46

Andersson, Charles John, 20

Angola, 72, 73; Namibian refugees in, 74; South African troops in, 75

Apartheid: and church structures, 59, 143; ecumenical opposition to, 83; established by law, 66–69; ethically neutral, 83, 98, 99; Kameeta on, 119, 122; opposed by Anglicans, 95; opposed by Lutherans, 87–92, 101; religious rationale for, 78; supported by Lutherans, 85; a theological issue, 101, 102, 119, 146; and violence, 95, 163 n.64

"Appeal to Lutheran Christians in Southern Africa," 100–104, 147–51 (Appendix)

Arendt, Hannah, 24, 159 n.22

Auala, Bp. Leonard, 86, 92

Augsburg Confession, 84; Apology to, 89

Barmen, Germany, 106

Barth, Karl, 98, 141, 162 n.40

Black theology, 115

Boesak, Allan, 115, 122

Bondelswart revolt, 35, 37

Bonhoeffer, Dietrich, 122

Botha, P. W., 97

Bravinck, H. J., 146

Bridgman, Jon M., 35

British Empire, 81, 83

Calvinism, 76, 77, 159 n.5

Calvinist state, 83

Cao, Diago, 18

Capitalism, introduction into Namibia, 55, 56

Cassinga massacre, 73

Civil religion, 77

Communism, 71, 75

Community, Church of (Oruuano), 85

Constructive engagement, 75

Council of Churches in Namibia, 71; membership in, 162 n.31; Open Letters, 96, 97, 109

Creation, orders of, 78, 79

Cuban linkage, 97

Democratic theory, 143

de Vries, Johannes L., 52

Dog tax, 62

Dualistic theology, 25, 78, 144

Dumeni, Bp. Kleopas, 71, 109, 110

Dutch Reformed Church, 85

Ecclesiology: African, 142; ethical focus, 104; mission of, 103; reconciliation and, 110; suffering and, 107

171